ST

MISE

TAKE
TIME FOR
SUNSETS

TAKE TIME FOR SUNSETS

Lester Bach O.F.M. Cap.

FRANCISCAN HERALD PRESS
Chicago, Illinois 60609

Take Time for Sunsets by Lester Bach O.F.M. Cap., copyright©1975 by Franciscan Herald Press, 1434 West 51st St., Chicago, Illinois 60609.

Library of Congress Cataloging in Publication Data:

Bach, Lester.
    Take time for sunsets.

    Bibliography: p.
    Includes index.
    1. Christian life—Catholic authors. 2. Francesco d'Assisi, Saint, 1182-1226. I. Title.
BX2350.2.B27   248'.48'2   75-1496
ISBN 0-8199-0565-8

NIHIL OBSTAT:
    Mark Hegener O.F.M.
    Censor

IMPRIMATUR:
    Msgr. Richard A. Rosemyer, J.D.
    Vicar General, Archdiocese of Chicago

MADE IN THE UNITED STATES OF AMERICA

Preface

TO UNDERSTAND FRANCIS and the Franciscan way, one must know of Francis. Placing him in historical perspective, being aware of the chronology of events in his life is not enough. More importantly, there is a moving spirit, a charism, that is the essence of Francis. One can feel this spirit in the pages of Father Bach's book. Through the sensitive words of one of Francis' own, we can feel our hearts stirring with a need, indeed a longing, to be intimate with Christ through the way of the "Little Ones".

The way of Francis is simply the gospel way. A spontaneous acceptance of all that the gospel life entails, with an enthusiasm sustained by hope and love. A way tempered by a poverty of the spirit; a dying to oneself that is epitomized in the prayer of Francis: "My God and my All."

In words a searching soul can relate to, we are led to the practicability of Francis. To simply respond with an open and full heart to the love of God. But how to open that heart—this is the problem, the reality that Father Bach addresses.

To follow Francis is to joyfully undertake that which leads to the Father. This joy is a pervading element of the Franciscan spirit. In these pages it is made evident by the positive acceptance of the "self" that may be trying to grow or develop in the process of getting to know Christ. The optimism rooted in real faith that whatever is attempted is possible, when done in the name of the Lord.

> Gratefully in Francis
> Patricia Larsen
> Merrillville, Ind.
> January 1, 1975

Foreword

THE GENESIS OF A BOOK is a mysterious thing to me. I suppose many people just sit down and write. I am certain many books come into being this way. But I know that this book did not happen that way. It started from seeds sown in my life by people I grew to love. It began in simple get-together sessions with people seeking Christ through the way of Francis of Assisi. It did not come to life full-blown and ready for print. It is the result of many long hours of discussion with good friends who love Francis of Assisi and who love Jesus Christ. Somewhere—in many years of sharing with friends . . . at a workshop in Joliet . . . at a convention in Santa Clara . . . in quiet moments with people in need . . . in painful moments of conflict . . . in the inner workings of the Third Order Fraternities in Northwest Indiana . . . through inner struggles of my own—from all of this has come this book.

It has been read and re-read; written and re-written. Now it is supposedly ready for printing. But it is not complete. Each day and month and year of life wants to add to it. But somewhere and at some time the additions cease and the book is frozen into words on the printed page. There is a kind of wonder in that, yet also disappointment because what is still growing in me is captured at one moment. Next year I will say things differently and see things more fully. How fleeting is time and how quickly the Lord continues to teach us and draw us to more intimacy. This book makes me painfully aware of that as well as the limitations of human language in describing our love affair with the Lord.

Only Jesus can write a living book. Mine is simply the reflections from this time in my life. It will pass by and yet this moment of sharing is important. Some of the truth is here. It may, perhaps, draw you to seek more of the truth who is Jesus. That would make me happy.

To the many Lay-Franciscans in different parts of the country who have encouraged me—Thank you! To the Lay-Franciscans of Northwest Indiana, this is our book. You and I have lived it together. Thank you!

To you, the reader, deal gently with these words. Not because I am soft and want no critique, but rather because I wish for you the gentleness of Jesus. Such gentleness will bring you to joy and life. May it always be yours as together we *Take Time For Sunsets*.

LESTER BACH O.F.M. Cap.

Acknowledgements

WE GRATEFULLY ACKNOWLEDGE the following publishers and authors for their permission to use quotations from their publications.

To the Franciscan Institute of St Bonaventure University for permission to use quotations from the magazine, *The Cord*.

To the Franciscan Herald Press for quotations from the following publications:

Marginals by Sister Mary Francis P.C.C.
Words of St Francis by Fr James Meyer O.F.M.
Writings of St Francis by Fahey-Hermann O.F.M.
Living our Future by van Galli S.J.
Wisdom of the Poverello by Leclerc

To Ave Maria Press for quotations from the book: *I Confess* by Father Buckley.

To Fides Publishers for a quotation from *Credo* by Louis Evely.

To Franciscan Publishers, Pulaski, Wis. for quotations from *Our life with God* by Fr Constantine Koser O.F.M.

To Paulist Press for quotations from *Christian approach to the Bible* by Dom Charlier.

To Argus Communications for a quotation from *A reason to live, a reason to die* (Copyright 1972)—John Powell S.J.

To Harper and Row for quotations from *Revolution of hope* by Eric Fromm.

To Harcourt Brace Jovanovich Inc. for quotations from the *Little Prince* by Antoine de Saint-Exupery.

To Doubleday and Company Inc. for the following book quotations:

Mr Blue by Myles Connolly
In the Spirit, in the flesh by Eugene Kennedy
Religion and personality by Van Kaam
Hope is the remedy by Bernard Haring
Where I found Christ by John O'Brien (editor)
St Francis of Assisi by G. K. Chesterton
Velveteen Rabbit by Margery Williams
All biblical quotations are from *The New American Bible.*

Fr. LESTER BACH O.F.M. Cap.

Contents

**TAKE
TIME FOR
SUNSETS**

1. On Being 'Me'

THE NIGHT WAS DARK. His spirit was depressed. The anticipation he had in prison, dreaming of this moment, was a
far-off memory. Now he, Francis Bernadone, was free! How
he had longed for this moment. How he had looked forward
to riding again in the hills and valleys around his home town
of Assisi. But the year in prison had changed him. He was
different. The music of the beautiful hillside no longer
touched and melted his mood. Things that had formerly
brought joy seemed quite empty and pointless now. It was a
frightening discovery. A point of discovery about his very
own self.

Self-discovery . . . the necessary but fearful adventure into
oneself. As we begin to learn about Francis of Assisi's way of
life, we will begin within ourselves. Building up a life of
dedication will need to start with self-acceptance. Our relationship with Jesus and with other people will be hindered if
we do not appreciate our own worth. We will *not* seek the
ad-man's "image-making" process. Rather, we will try simply
to explore the reality of 'me.' A look at my personal love of
Jesus that will push me to mature into the best possible
'me' so that I might be a finely tuned instrument in
His hands.

YOU ARE GOOD

At the heart of my own beliefs about people is the
conviction that each of us is 'good.' You are made in the

image of God who does not make useless or evil things.

> Let us make man in our image, after our likeness. Let them have dominion over the fish of the sea, the birds of the air, and the cattle, and over all the wild animals and all the creatures that crawl on the ground . . . God looked at everything he had made and he found it very good.
>
> Genesis 1: 26 - 31

You are good! This is the reality we start with, the idea that man is fundamentally good. God has created him as someone of worth.

Some people find it hard to accept this idea. We have been told in many different ways that we are not good. We have often acted on the presumption that we would be bad unless we were directed to the good. The "Don't do this!" and "Don't do that!!" made us feel that our natural desires would lead to evil rather than to good. So many of us begin life with a negative self-image. It is not easy to erase such feelings.

When we say that 'you are good,' we mean to deny the opposite. But we are not saying you are perfect. There is a gap between the good you know you ought to do and what you actually do. When we say you are good, we are not saying you never make poor choices or bad decisions. Neither are we saying that you are already a saint waiting in line for canonization. We all know that there is much room for growth and improvement in our lives.

What we are saying is that you have a good foundation. God made you in his image and that image is a good one. You are good because God made you so. You may mis-use or mis-direct this goodness in many foolish ways. You may fail and you may sin. But you have a fundamental goodness that can grow and blossom and overcome the evil.

When we accept this idea we have a different perspective

on the spiritual life. We all know that there are obstacles and barriers within us that keep Jesus' Spirit from operating freely in our lives. But instead of thinking only that we must knock down these obstacles so that Jesus can *get in*, this view is saying that we knock down the walls within us in order to let the goodness out. If we feel that we are bad and goodness must come from the outside in, we can become too concerned with externals. Things like dealing with difficult people; handling temptations; keeping the rules of the game; external conformity of all kinds. When we look at ourselves as good, it becomes a matter of recognizing that only an inner change will free that goodness in us. We can no longer be satisfied with removing external obstacles to growth. Now we must peel away the false pride and selfishness that lives within us and keeps us from using our God-given goodness.

Such an idea is not meant to throw out the old. Externals too have a place in our lives and external obstacles have to be dealt with. But now we know that the externals are not 'everything.'

In fact, our heart tells us that the internal obstacles are the more mountainous ones. Moreover, we start with a solid hope that we can meet these obstacles and overcome them because of God's presence within us. Right at the beginning we know who our savior is going to be. It is Jesus and the power of his Spirit and no other. We can be good because we already possess the seed of goodness.

Sometimes we dream about the person we might be. "If only I were like Chris . . . or Jon." We struggle to accept ourselves, to be happy to be 'me.' This is an important part of our pilgrimage to Jesus. *If* we accept ourselves, we can begin to deal more realistically with life's problems. We can set goals and reach out to others. We do not need to hide behind masks of aggressiveness or shyness or defensiveness of various kinds. As we come to accept ourselves, we can accept the fact that living will bring risks. But we will face life and not run from it.

We need the help of others to do this. We need someone to say to us that we are good. We need to be able to say, to ourselves and to another: "I'm OK, you're OK." Much of this feeling of being OK will depend on the support and honesty of true friends who say it to us.

Jesus put it this way: "Love your neighbor as yourself." We need the support of our neighbor to feel good about ourselves—but our neighbor needs the same support from us. It has to be an honest telling. Exaggeration or made-up compliments will do nothing. If we honestly believe in the core goodness of man, then we can affirm this goodness in others even when they may make poor decisions or do stupid things. Our personal experience tells us that we need to be told repeatedly before we believe that we are good. Self-acceptance is never achieved in isolation, but is at least partially dependent on others. We, in turn, must give such support to others.

Loving oneself properly is important to living a good life. We need to accept the good things about ourselves without getting big-headed about it. We need to recognize and appreciate our feelings. We need to assess evaluations that others give us about ourselves and wisely integrate that truth into our self-image. At the root of the healthy and holy person is a well-adjusted person, able to receive love and trust as well as giving it. Anyone who wishes to follow the Franciscan way of life must be a healthy person, possessing a solid self-image.

It is good to read about Francis of Assisi and see how un-self-conscious he was. Life was too full of living to worry about how he looked to others. He compared himself with Jesus. This model of comparison always called for a 'stretching' of his spirit to reach out to the Son of God. Such stretching made him a very complete and whole person indeed.

ANOTHER APPROACH

We can look at life from still another perspective. We

might examine the things that most often move us to action. We use the term 'value' to describe such influences. Webster tells us that "to value something" is to think highly of it, to esteem it and prize it. We 'value' a good investment, a tasty meal of our favorite food, a good sporting event. We may value being 'real people' as defined by the Skin Horse in the *Velveteen Rabbit*: "It doesn't happen all at once. You become. It takes a long time. That's why it doesn't happen to people who break easily or have sharp edges or who have to be carefully kept."

For our purposes, value requires not only that you *say* that you value something, but also that you *do* something because of the value. If you were to list things or ideas or people whom you 'value,' you might well ask yourself: "When was the last time I acted on this value or did something for the person I say I value?" We would call it a real value only if you acted on it consistently and with pride.

Values, of course, are subject to change. Experience brings certain values to the fore in our lives. Different things become more important as we move on in life. But values will be a directing force in our lives. What is important to us (what we value) will move us to action. There are a few things that it is important to know about our kind of 'values.'

Values must be chosen freely and without being forced on us. When I am forced to do something, it is not really a value, because I have no choice in the matter. Eating, for example, is not a value. If I want to live, I need to eat. However, I do have a choice about *what* I eat and I might value one food over another. A value must be freely chosen from among alternatives. They do not come pre-packaged nor are they the result of impulsive choices. On the contrary, since they touch so much of life, they are given thoughtful consideration. Should I, for example, choose the gospel value of 'loving my enemy,' I also accept the work this requires, the forgiveness I have to show and any other consequence.

Such a decision requires thoughtful and prayerful consideration.

Values will be cherished. If they are important to me, I will be willing to stand up for them publicly. I will follow them consistently and with conviction. Sporadic acceptance of any value says that I do not really cherish it and it is, at best, a very weak influence. A real value will move me to consistent action and a ready acceptance of all the consequences of the value.

Look at the things or persons you claim to value. Hobbies, organizations, people, beliefs, possessions, ideals, patterns of action you claim as values. Check to see if you have chosen them from several options open to you. Do you really cherish them and show it? Do you accept the consequences of embracing the value? Do they consistently move you to action? Honest evaluation sometimes reveals that we have very few real values. If we wish to follow the Franciscan way of life, we will need solid, Christian, gospel values.

Other things are sometimes called values. A goal in life is important. It gives direction to life and clarifies the things we hope to achieve. If we organize our lives to attain that goal, it has at least some characteristics of a value. Attitudes are sometimes called values. They indicate that we are for or against some person, idea or thing. Attitudes can serve as indicators of values. Basic interests and feelings are sometimes called values. Both are reactions to life. But they are generally too temporary to label as true values. Beliefs or convictions that move us to consistent action are similar to values. Actions speak louder than words. But it need not always be so. Some people attend Church regularly and consistently without ever being really committed to the values of Jesus. Such activity may be mere social conformity and no value at all. On the other hand, if such action springs from an inner commitment to Jesus, the beliefs and/or convictions are real values.

SOOOOO

Examining my values opens the door to a better understanding of what makes 'me' tick. In coming to the Franciscan way of life, a choice will have to be made. You will need to choose this way of coming to Jesus in preference to other ways. It is not the only way nor is it the way everyone will choose. But if you choose this way of life, then you must value it. You will need to follow it consistently, openly, and cherish your calling to follow Francis. You will need to accept all the consequences of your choice and follow it proudly. Half-way measures or half-hearted response will do nothing but destroy the call of God to follow the Franciscan way of life.

Developing this kind of valued dedication is not a product that is produced after a certain length of time. It is a process that will continue for as long as you follow this way of life. There is no magic here, no easy formulas that work easy transformations. This way of life requires effort, consistent and persistent effort. It will require, especially as you begin, an honesty about that wonderful, mysterious, silly, wise, mask-filled and open person known by your name.

There are no automatic rules. God goes about this in his own way which is often quite unexpected. But the beginnings are within us. The direction and distance you may travel will be determined by your generosity. Should you choose to follow the Franciscan way of life, your search will never end. There will be constant new beginnings as self is better understood and the gospel becomes more alive for you. It will not be a black-and-white world. Self-searching and seeking God involves darkness as well as light coupled with long stretches of grey. There will be uncomfortable facts about 'self' that you will have to deal with. There will be delightful discoveries of the good things that are part of you. It will be an exploration of discovery that will be exhilarating, exasperating, joyful, painful, frustrating, uplifting, depressing and delightful, but never boring. Like good pilgrims, we will travel on.

If we refuse to face our real self; if we keep hiding behind masks of defensiveness, we shall be like a Hollywood movie set—looking good on the outside, but empty shells within. God calls us to wholeness. But he still waits on our free 'yes' to his call.

To walk such a path alone would be frightening. Our Franciscan way of life brings us to other people who are walking the same path. They are our companions in the search. We walk together in seeking Jesus. It will be joy-and-pain combined in the gentle paradox of living the gospel life. Jesus spoke to us his message of peace. He spoke of forgiveness from a cross of agony. He calls us to follow him to that cross. Francis of Assisi digested this message and made it his own. You and I stand ready to follow Francis' way to Jesus. Jesus' own words urge us on: "Seek and you shall find!"

2. On Top of Alverna

IT WAS ON A MOUNTAIN. Francis came here to be alone. Even Brother Leo, his best friend, was not with him here. Francis had come to La Verna to be totally alone with Jesus. What went through the mind and heart of Francis that night we do not know. But it was a night of intimate communing with Jesus. Francis understood well that the cross is the way to Jesus and he embraced the cross. On this mountain Francis asked the impossible (for those who do not know how to love). He asked to suffer as Jesus suffered and to burn with the love that burned in the heart of Jesus. On this mountain, in a moment of silent intimacy, the impossible happened.

Absorbed in prayer, Francis became aware that something was happening to him. His heart had never felt such powerful surging before. Never before had he recognized the depth of Jesus' "I thirst!" Nor had Francis ever felt such a human need for someone to care as Jesus must have experienced in his garden of agony. Never before had strength and weakness so pulsed in him. His heart was near to breaking as he experienced the agony of Jesus and shared the love that had broken the heart of Jesus. As Francis looked at his hands, he saw there the external marks of love, the marks of Jesus' own passion in his body. Love and suffering were gathered together to reflect the love and suffering of Calvary. On this mountain of La Verna, Calvary was once more a reality. Twelve hundred years had passed between the one and the other, but it was as though time had no meaning. In the silent power of that moment, the prayer that sprang from Francis' lips was simple, direct and total: "My God and my all!"

This moment in the life of Francis comes after twenty years of 'conversion.' It is important to know that. Very often we think of saints as ready-made, nicely bundled and ready for holiness at the drop of a hat. The truth is quite different.

The conversion of Francis of Assisi is unique. But that is true of all of us. We come to God in our own, unique way. But there are common elements though the combinations may differ.

Consider the situation Francis faced in his early twenties. The prestige thing of his time was to become a "Knight." It was the Cadillac mentality of the 13th century. God's influence on the lives of people seemed remote. The leadership in the Church left much to be desired. There was a spirit of restlessness in society. A passion for 'freedom' from domination by the rich and powerful was sweeping through society. In Assisi, this anti-feeling was directed toward a large castle that brooded over the city. It became the symbol of all the hated injustices people had to endure. The mood of violence and restlessness came to a head and this brooding castle was stormed and demolished. The stones from the castle were used to build a wall around Assisi. With this conquest, a sort of "we shall overcome" mentality rang through the streets and alleys of Assisi.

Francis grew up in this atmosphere. He had a deep passion for freedom and justice, but it was tempered by the influence of the romantic stories of knighthood and chivalry. The 'pop music' of the time played up to the virtues of the strong but compassionate knight-at-arms.

When God chose to communicate with Francis, he used the symbols of the 13th century. A castle, banners, shields, chivalry, knighthood. God spoke in symbols that Francis could understand—yet Francis also mis-read things, mistaking the symbols for reality. Little wonder that Francis' initial failures in seeking knighthood were such a blow to him. Like us, Francis struggled through a misunderstanding of the designs of God. Francis had to work his way through the hard experiences of suffering and failure, of confusion and fear.

What did the dream of the 20-year-old Francis look like? Francis could look forward to a rosy future. His father was a well-to-do cloth merchant in Assisi. Money was not a problem in the Bernadone family. Business looked good. Francis had more than enough spending money. Pietro Bernadone was proud of his son and indulged him. He enjoyed seeing Francis assume leadership in his group of friends. Francis had an attractive personality and the steady supply of spending money was no hindrance. One day, mused Pietro, this son would inherit the business. It did no harm to spoil him a little.

Francis himself enjoyed his position. He was always around when good times were happening in Assisi. Francis' dream of the future could well afford to be rosy. Reality supported his dreams. His personal blending of rousing joy and gentlemenly courtesy was a good combination. His personal dream of becoming a knight was well within the realm of possibility. When he finally rode out with the army of Assisi to do battle with the enemy town of Perugia, Francis was full of anticipation of glory.

Sad to say, Assisi's dreams were bigger and better than her army. Perugia roundly defeated the forces of Assisi. Many prisoners were captured by Perugia, among them, Francis Bernadone, son of Pietro Bernadone, the cloth merchant. His first ride into 'glory' had ended in defeat. Francis is just another prisoner of war.

Once again God establishes his pattern of doing the un-expected. Prison life was hard on Francis. Though his spirit was not broken, this is a depressing time for him. The imposed limitations of prison slowly changed Francis. He still dreamed of glory, but got the hee-haw when he shared his dreams with the other men. The other prisoners chalked it up to his youth and inexperience. They had heard such stories before. Besides, it was good for a laugh and laughter was hard to come by in prison.

Francis learned a number of important things in prison. His understanding of human nature grew. He sided with a man that most of the prisoners considered a traitor. He learned how rough men can be on someone like that. The closed prison community was harsh and direct in its judgement. Francis' feelings of compassion were tested in the crucible of ridicule and mockery. Francis paid the price and matured in the process.

A year is a long time—day after weary day in confinement. Body and spirit suffer in loneliness and inactivity. Prisons do not develop sunshine spirits. Men grew bitter as the days passed. Their spirit depressed Francis. It was an important year in terms of Francis' conversion, but he could see little of that at the moment.

Finally, negotiations led to a freeing of the prisoners. The men of Assisi were freed to return home. But what does it mean to be free? Francis had longed for this day. Now that it was upon him he was quiet. He was free to walk the mountain trails and drink in the quiet beauty around him. Good times with friends were eagerly anticipated. He could again pursue his dreams. He was free!

The night was dark. His spirit was depressed. All of the anticipation seemed like a long lost memory. Francis had expected things to be the same, once he was free again. They were not. A year had changed many things. Francis was not certain what had happened, but everything was different now. The things that used to bring him joy were empty now. He felt isolated and alone and a little frightened.

He was still ill from his prison weakness. At home he spent much time alone. Often he would ride out alone into the hills around Assisi. At parties he was often quiet and pensive. Gradually his awareness of life returned, different than before and stronger. A dilapidated little Church became a place to rest and reflect. It was un-visited and the old priest was kind to him. He was haunted by many questions, but slowly he came to a feeling of peace. The struggle was not over, not by any means, but he discovered a new strength inside himself. Then events seemed to point out an answer to his struggles. Another army was being raised to fight in Sicily. Another opportunity for knighthood and glory.

For a second time Francis leaves Assisi. But once again God pursued Francis with unexpected happenings. Shortly after leaving Assisi, Francis fell ill. As he rested in the room of an Inn, he experienced God's presence. "Who can do more for you, Francis, the Lord or the Servant?" "The Lord." Francis replied. The voice responded: "Then why do you leave the Lord for the servant? The prince for the vassal?" "What do you want me to do?" Francis asked. "Return to Assisi and what you are to do will be revealed to you there."

The words puzzled Francis. Only a short while before he had dreamed of a great castle filled with shields and swords. He took this as a confirmation of his dream of becoming a knight. Now it all seemed turned to ashes. It was a weary, sick and perplexed young man who returned to Assisi.

No welcome greeted his arrival. Just whispered comments and a lot of knowing looks as he rode into the city. Just another blow-hard who couldn't measure up when the going got tough. Francis himself had to face a much deeper and more serious struggle inside himself than he had ever known before.

Francis says little about these days. He does not mention them as the point of his conversion. Neither does he define the hours spent in reflection in his cave as the point of conversion. He admits his fears and weakness in facing his father. But in his writings none of these are marked as the time when he understood what was happening. It took a moment, a symbol, to bring all of this together in his mind.

Francis was riding in the open country. A sense of freedom caught him as the horse galloped along the dusty road. The breeze in his face was refreshing and the beauty of the hills gave him a sense of well being. It was a beautiful day to be alive!

Then, bright as the sun in the road before him, was a leper! A leper, symbol of evil and rejection and disfiguration. The joy, the freedom of a moment before drained from Francis. He stopped short before that white, sore-covered, horrible man who stood there in his path. Francis was trapped. For in his mind the words of Jesus rang out: "Love your neighbor as yourself!" Too many gospel words clanged to the forefront of his attention.

"Run! Get away!" cried one part of Francis. "Kiss him!" came another cry within. Francis shuttered at the completeness of the demands. It was as though time and the world stood still and only he and the leper lived. Here it was, where logic and love must meet. Without a doubt he knew that his own 'wholeness' demanded that he kiss the leper. Yet every fiber of his feelings rebelled at the thought. It was an eternity caught up in a moment. It is a moment on which a whole life can hinge.

Francis knew what had to be done. Before he could persuade himself otherwise, he was off his horse, standing in front of that horribly deformed and stinking man, and he embraced him! Francis Bernadone had gotten off his high horse and thrown his arms around a leper!! Time was not. Francis only knew that he got back on his horse and rode away. When he looked back, the road was empty. Francis was changed. It is this moment that Francis points to as the moment of conversion:

> The Lord gave to me, Brother Francis, the grace of beginning to do penance in this way. When I was in sin, it seemed to me extremely distasteful to even look at lepers. The Lord himself led me among them, and I practiced mercy with them. And when I came away from them, what had seemed bitter to me was changed

to acceptance of spirit and body. After that I did not
wait long and put aside self-indulgence.

As we ride this open road with Francis and we too come
to a moment of truth, we shall be faced with a hard choice.
We may discover some of the fears that run parts of our life.
Fears that keep us from facing all the consequences of our
Franciscan calling. As we walk with Francis in the beginning
of his conversion, we know that the moment of the Stigmata
on La Verna cannot be understood without the dusty road
and the leper who stood there. Francis did not plot his
conversion. It came to him unexpectedly. Yet it faced him
with his personal fear and drew him to a personal honesty
that changed the direction of his life. He knew the options
and he chose to embrace the leper. He could have run away.
He chose not to.

Our own personal moment of truth may be stretched out
over days or months or years. In fact, we may put off ever
facing up to it. Yet, we will be free and whole only when we
face it and embrace the direction Jesus is leading. It will
change everything inside us. Whether we accept or refuse
Jesus' invitation, things will never again be the same. If we
refuse, that refusal will influence other decisions we shall
make. If we accept, we shall be called to accept the unexpected as commonplace. It is possible to hide from making
the decision and to use clever means to avoid it. No matter
what decision we make, we know what we are choosing.

When we say "Yes" to his call, the Lord will ask things
of us that we had never dreamed of doing. We shall never
again find room in life for bogging down in self-pity nor
ever again forgetting that our power is in the Spirit of God
and not in ourselves. Jesus will call us to intimacy and
human words will be too clumsy to describe it. He will ask
us to Calvary and we will follow him there. He will lead us
up Mt. Tabor and we will celebrate with him there. Little by
little, with a gentle persuasion, he will lead us to the

commitment of La Verna. We will seek to feel both the love and the pain of the Lord so that we might be one with him. We will do that because it is the way of Francis, and this is our call.

It might be easier for us if we refuse the call right now. But once Jesus has touched us and called us to the Franciscan way of life, there is within us a deep longing that needs to say "Yes." In the embrace expressed by our 'yes,' we will find that what we thought would be bitter will be turned into sweetness of soul and body.

3. Who Can I Turn To?

ONCE WE BELIEVE IN OURSELVES, we find that we can take the risks of a child. Things like wonder and curiosity, delight and tears, spontaneous loving and quiet hurting can be revealed. My problem in writing this book is that everything is neatly divided into chapters. Life does not really come in chapters. Life is not meant to be cut up and divided into neat little compartments. Man is meant to be whole, complete and integrated.

Faith in Jesus is an important element of integrated living. The words are important: faith - in - Jesus. It is a very personal relationship of which we speak. Faith is not simply a listing of doctrines that I believe. Neither is it merely the intellectual assent to the truth of dogmas of the Church. Theology can seek such an assent. Theology can expand on the meaning of faith-truths. But faith itself is more than that. Faith means coming in touch with Jesus and allowing him to touch us.

It is in Christ and through his blood that we have been redeemed and our sins forgiven, so immeasureably generous is God's favor to us . . . In Him we were chosen; for in the decree of God, who administers everything according to his will and counsel, we were predestined to praise his glory by being the first to hope in Christ. In him you too were chosen, when you heard the glad tidings of salvation, the word of truth, and believed in it, you were sealed with the Holy Spirit

19

who had been promised.

Ephesians 2: 7 - 13

Our salvation comes through Christ who is the head of all things.

Faith is our personal relationship with Jesus that leads to following him wherever he leads. The demands of real faith outstrip anything that legalism or dogmas could require. Faith requires, ultimately, an absolutely total response. It is a relationship that seeks an ever deeper intimacy. It sets no limits or conditions to the giving over of self. In the last analysis it shall require everything of us.

Faith, then, is not just knowledge, although knowledge enriches faith. Faith is a covenant relationship with Jesus, binding us to him in a personal pact. Covenant means 'coming together.' Our covenant faith means coming together in trusting friendship with Jesus. It is not a superior-subject relationship. It is a sharing of life, all of life. Our Lord told us at the Last Supper that we are no longer servants, but friends. Friends establish bonds with each other. Faith is our bond with the living, risen Jesus who is the way, the truth and the life.

On our part we bring ourselves to this relationship. We come to it with our hang-ups, our insecurities, our pride, our rationalisms, our technological gods, our joy, our capabilities and everything that makes us who we are. The kind of person I am will have some effect on the relationship. It is 'me' who will have to open the door of my life to Jesus. It is 'me' who must accept the consequences of this deeply personal faith in Jesus. The more open I am to Jesus, the more responsive I am to him, the deeper will be my faith.

Today, there are many different ideas about Jesus. Not all of them are correct. Each of us has our own image of Jesus that may need changing. We must be aware that faith requires knowing and loving the real Jesus and not some figment of our imagination or a Jesus that fits into ideas that are simply comfortable. Jesus is the man who transformed the life of Francis. If we would follow Francis, we must constantly seek the face of Jesus as he really is.

WHO IS JESUS?

The seeking of the answer to that question will take us through valleys of darkness as well as to heights of revelation. A few things are important to consider to clear the air of some false ideas about Jesus.

Jesus is not the feminine man of so many pictures and holy cards. Jesus is a man. He is a man in everything except sin. Jesus had the eminently common sense not to destroy his human gifts by the poor choice that sin offers. Jesus is human. I relate to Jesus the man and through him come to know the Father. Jesus is not simply someone who was human back in the year one. He is human now! In his glorified body he is still human. When we consider this fact we can be assured that Jesus does not have to imagine what it is like to be human. He simply has to remember. He showed this after the resurrection. He ate with his friends. Thomas the doubter touched him and felt him. He possessed particular powers proper to a glorified body, but he took pains to reveal that he is still the human Jesus, risen from the dead. It is through the 'sacrament' of his humanness that he will lead us to the Father. Faith relates to the human Jesus, real, alive and present in the 'now' in which I live.

As we grow in relationships with others, we come to a deeper understanding of the way another thinks, the way he looks at things, the perspective he has on life, the attitudes and values that move him to action. If we are honest we find that we may have imposed certain attitudes and images on Jesus. We easily come to a conclusion that we enjoy and then seek to find a way of having Jesus say what we want to hear. As long as we refuse to let loose of our false 'images of Jesus,' our faith will stagnate. When we are responsive to Jesus as he really is, our relationship will grow.

Sometimes we have made Jesus a magician who will solve everything for us. At other times we have made him a stern judge with spies everywhere to catch us in evil. Or we may have made him into some gentle nobody who wouldn't hurt anyone. And we even push him into accepting our sinning on the plea that he will 'understand.' He does; and that may be uncomfortable for us. In short, we need to be aware of the many false Jesus-images we may have and begin to erase them.

Perhaps these images are understandable. For long years we have spent little time with the Scriptures. Many people might still live with the fear that to read and respond to Scripture is to put oneself on the threshold of heresy. Yet the real Jesus is revealed in his written Word. It is in the Scriptures that we discover Jesus; his way of dealing with people; his way of looking at life; his response to suffering and death and betrayal. Like Francis of Assisi, we shall need to find Jesus in the Gospel. The Holy Spirit led Francis to the heights of prayer and holiness, but it began and was built up on the Scriptures:

> And after the Lord gave me some brothers, there was nobody to show me what to do; but the most High himself revealed to me that I was to live according to the form of the Holy Gospel.
>
> *Words of St. Francis*, #282c

Our call to the Franciscan way of life will likewise bring us to the Scriptures. The gospels are our way of life!

Thoughtful reflection on the Scriptures can give me a knowledge of Jesus. I can sense the way he felt in different situations. I can learn how he reacted to different kinds of people. I can capture some sense of his prayer; his hopes and dreams; his human frustrations. The Scriptures will make me more deeply aware of Jesus as a person, which in turn will present an opportunity for deepened faith in Jesus. After the resurrection we see Jesus continuing his concern for his friends. His delicacy in handling the fear of the apostles. His strong sense of leadership in commissioning his friends to do his work. His promise to remain with them always. All of this tells me of the relationship he seeks with me. His gospel 'Word' helps me to know him better. Reflective reading of scripture will bring deeper insight into this man-God whom I wish to love and follow. My persistence and constancy in coming to this written "Word of the Lord" will bring me to deeper friendship with the Word-made-flesh.

The way this happens in the life of any one individual cannot be computerized into a 'do-it-yourself' program. As your faith grows, so will your yearning for deeper union. Your seeking will lead you to take more time for Jesus in prayerful communing. As your awareness of Jesus grows, you shall yield yourself to Him more and more. Your life changes as you move to greater 'handing over' to him.

As this responsiveness gains momentum in our lives, we grow more totally integrated, putting faith and life together. The scriptures give us his living Word. But the scriptures are not the only way in which he reveals himself. We find Jesus in Liturgy and Sacrament and most especially in the Eucharist. Jesus is present in Eucharist giving us the sign of life. In Eucharist he shows us again that he loves us even when it requires his death and he challenges us to imitate him. Jesus is present through our contact with people. He comes to us in the people whom he has called to a covenant relationship. All of these contacts deepen our relationship with Jesus in faith. No one of them can do everything. Yet the fullness of faith shall always be found in the Eucharist and in the Word.

What all this means is that, in the process of faith, our greatest need is constantly to revise our own concept of God, who is infinitely greater and more loving than our

finite minds can possibly grasp.
A reason to live, a reason to die John Powell, 192

We all grow older without doing anything except staying alive. But age does not automatically bring wisdom. We must seek wisdom with vigorous effort.

> Life gives you pretty much what you give it. She gives beauty to those who try to add to her beauty. She gives happiness to those who share their happiness with her. She gives, even, love to those who love her. But these are very, very few. Almost all of us have a capacity for being loved. But few of us have a capacity for loving.
>
> *Mr Blue* Myles Connally, 72

Our present day need for Jesus is enormously obvious. Man often feels alienated, alone, overwhelmed by forces that seem beyond his control. The obstacles to belief today may differ, yet the human need is the same. We have a deep craving not to be alone. We want acceptance badly. We want to grow as full human persons. We need someone we can trust, someone who can be trusted with the innermost secrets and aches and joys of our heart. We long for the friendship of Jesus. Since we are called to immortality, we will never quite be satisfied with human friendships. The unending friendship and acceptance by Jesus can satisfy our human longing.

> I want you to know how hard I am struggling for you and for the Laodiceans and the many others who have never seen me in the flesh. I wish their hearts to be strengthened and themselves to be closely united in love, enriched with full assurance by their knowledge of the mystery of God—namely Christ—in whom every treasure of wisdom and knowledge is hidden . . .

In Christ the fullness of deity resides in bodily form.
Yours is a share in this fullness, in him who is the head
of every principality and power.

Colossians 2: 1 - 3 & 9 - 10

The Franciscan way of life is full of Jesus. He is at its
heart. Francis of Assisi knew Jesus and took him seriously.
We are called to do likewise. Our search is aided by our
Franciscan calling. It will require constant searching for
Jesus in our lives. He will continue to change and re-direct
our lives. He shall bring us to his cross and raise us to life in
resurrection again and again on the journey. But it is the
'real' life. It is the gospel life. Truly, we shall overcome for
the Lord is with us.

4. A Disturbing Development

The man living by the gospels does not just do things
for others, nor does he just pray for them while
remaining at some distance from their troubles and
hopes. The Christian lives with the world, bridging the
gap between himself and others through active empathy
. . . he is able to live and move with others in a sensitive
and understanding way. A man fleshes out his own
gospel incarnation through being able to hear and grasp
the experience of other persons.

In the spirit, in the flesh Kennedy 107

FRANCIS BERNADONE NEEDED TO GROW in his faith-relationship with Jesus. The search of Francis reflects our own
search to know the living Jesus. I want to share my own
'seeing' of Francis' search. I am not overly concerned about
chronological order so much as emotional order. I would
like to have you feel with Francis as he struggles through
his conversion.

When Francis was freed from the Perugian prison, he was
at loose ends with life. He had no special plans about his
life-style, no big dreams about the meaning of life. He had
friends, money, time, entertainment. What he lacked was
direction in life. He wasn't totally bored with life, but
neither did he have things 'together.' Another failure in
seeking knighthood left him puzzled and frustrated and
empty inside.

There are several possible options in such a situation. He

could pour out his energies in a rash of activity and good times to quiet the turmoil inside or, at least, to escape its voice. Or he could withdraw from people and wallow in self-pity or take time for reflection. Francis seems to have combined these options. He still engaged in the good times with his friends, but he also became much more thoughtful and reflective. We do not know all the thoughts that passed through his mind. But his personal experience of the presence of God remained with him. The dream or vision or whatever term you might use to describe his experience in the Inn, remained with him. Somehow, he had to understand what it meant to 'serve the Lord and not the servant.'

Francis is caught at a crossroads in his life. It was a time between action and reflection; a time between moving out in trust and holding back in fear. His faith in Jesus was growing but Jesus was not revealing any blueprints. Jesus was silent. Pietro, Francis' father, often grew impatient with the listlessness of his son. Father and son may often have engaged in arguments about this seeming laziness and dreaminess in Francis. It is a time of turmoil for Francis.

Obviously this is 'filling-in' the gaps between the historical facts about Francis. But given Francis' temperament and that of his father, it seems realistic. Francis was volatile and patient; impulsive and pensive; forgiving and ready to dispute things. His father had a different perspective of life and had the same strong characteristics. The ingredients for conflict between these two men are obvious. Within Francis there is a struggle with the message of a God who has grown very silent.

Francis searches for some light out of this dark cave. He feels a deep need to pray. He cannot dismiss God. Jesus is someone who is alive now! How often he rides out to the little church of San Damiano to pray before the crucifix. As God's message becomes more clear, the struggle to say a complete 'yes' to everything the Lord asks becomes more difficult.

It is a frightening time for Francis. A terrible warfare tears at his spirit as he struggles to accept the call of Jesus. The struggle is not a simple, smooth and easy slide to acceptance. Too many writers make conversion stories sound like embraceable trips through enchanted lands. It is never so and it was not so with Francis. His father's angry intervention in this struggle; the angry 'grounding' of his son; the conflict between them, closes in on Francis. What deep feelings must have existed between these two men. Both had great ambition, but what different directions that ambition took. Fear of his father's wrath drove Francis into hiding. He spent long days and weeks away from home. But how this must have added to his agony of spirit, torn between the call of Jesus and his love for his parents. How often, huddled in his cold cave, did the cold winds of depression and exhaustion bite at his spirit. Again and again he puzzled over the same ideas and tried to analyze the ways of loving. Such an experience leaves its mark on a man. But it also finally led to decision, a decision to say "yes" to Jesus.

When we read such words, I wonder if we appreciate the emotional and spiritual struggle of this gentle, buoyant young man from Assisi. A man as sensitive as Francis would be torn to bits in such a struggle. We know how it ended and it sounds so simple. But we will not know Francis if we look only to the conclusion and never walk with him in struggling to that conclusion.

We know that he accepted Lady Poverty and began to repair the Church of San Damiano. That is what the voice from the crucifix had said: "Repair my Church!" We know what a snicker this new action brought to the townsfolk of Assisi. We know that he was made fun of, mocked and taunted every time he ventured into Assisi to beg. He was that 'crazy' Bernadone boy!

The decision was made, his 'yes' given. But the consequences still had to be faced. Francis could not forget the pain he saw in his father's face. How he loved that man.

Friends could not understand and how could he explain? How strange that his acceptance of Jesus' call should bring such fracturing and pain in those who were so close to his heart. He still walked in a dark night. How difficult to face the rejection of his father; the look of confusion and love in the eyes of his mother; to experience the condescension of his friends. This is the path of conversion for Francis. Hardly a flower strewn path filled with joy-joy-joy. Such is the price of his irrevocable decision to believe in Jesus Christ.

Other consequences were not slow in coming. For Pietro Bernadone it was one thing to put up with youthful shenanigans, but when this young son starts selling cloth and gives the money away; when he makes a fool of the Bernadone family, that is just too much! Knowing the character of these two men, Francis and Pietro, it was only a matter of time before a confrontation would occur. Pietro would be pushed no farther. He initiated civil proceedings to regain the money Francis had given away. Francis demanded that the trial take place before the Bishop, since he considered himself a servant of the Church. So the Bishop's court became the place of confrontation.

How can we describe this public trial between father and son? Are all the facts so clear-cut and the issues so boldly proclaimed that we can easily take sides? As Pietro and Francis faced each other, did they both feel that they were right? These two men facing each other and both of them miserably poor. Francis had embraced poverty with a passion; Pietro, who had lost a son and his self-esteem in one grand gesture. Pietro won the court case. Francis is guilty as charged. There was no doubt of that. Yet, of the two men in that court, Pietro had lost. How often, I wonder, in his sleepless nights, did this proud man hear the echo of Francis' words: "Until now I have called Pietro Bernadone my father. But now I say only: 'Our Father in heaven.' "

Francis speaks only in cautious terms of this moment in his life. He does not gloat over this moment of confrontation with a man he loves. The gesture in that courtroom made his commitment public and final. The gospel requires such finality. But it must have been a special cross in the memory of Francis. We know of no reconciliation between father and son. We are not told of any future meetings between Francis and Pietro. But in all those times of prayer on Alvernia, Francis must have often remembered his father. In the days to come, when Francis was acclaimed by the people of Assisi, is it too much to imagine Pietro on the fringes of the crowd, wanting to reach out to this son of his? Mere conjecture, but certainly possible. Francis is drawn to Jesus in an intimacy that ends in crucifixion and resurrection. Francis' love would not have narrowed along this way. It could only expand and embrace, above all, the man who had given him the name Francesco.

It is through struggles such as these that Francis came to know the living Jesus. He was more deeply aware of the 'presence' of Jesus.

How does anyone describe 'presence'? It is not simply physical closeness. People in an elevator are physically close but need not be 'present' to each other at all. Presence does not require that I am so interested in someone that I must probe the deepest recesses of their heart. Letting everything out and hurling it at another is not the way of presence. Real presence is something more subtle and gentle than that. It is what happens when a husband and wife can look across a room of people and be one. It happens when two friends meet after a long separation and simply linger in an embrace of silence. It happens when faith lightens a path that seems so dark by a simple 'feel' in faith of the presence of Jesus. It is a gift of self to another with no strings attached. It springs from a living relationship.

Such a presence cannot be submitted to laboratory analysis. Expose it to the cold, impersonal investigation of the laboratory and it will dissipate. Presence cannot be 'put on' for the sake of scientific investigation. The signs of its presence speak in a language that words could only dull. To feel free and at ease with another, to be happy to be together is to experience presence. We do not earn it, it is a gift to us, freely given. You know it and you respond to it. You work to create that same presence for the other. Conversation becomes communication. We identify with the other person and relax in his acceptance. An encounter with real presence is etched deeply on the heart.

How did the 'presence' of Jesus develop in the life of Francis? Francis is much like we are. There was a time when he was satisfied with things as they were. He wasn't worried about finding a job. He had all the spending money he needed. He had good friends. He had a good personality and could lead people fairly well. He was probably considered quite 'normal.' We can presume he took some time for the Lord, but no more than any other 'normal' young man in Assisi. Francis, in his early 20's, was quite satisfied with life. Had things continued this way, he might have married, took over the family business, raised a family, been a local politician and lived a very 'normal' life. Like many good men he would have died, been mourned by family and friends, and then been forgotten by history.

But that did not happen. His search for knighthood ended in disaster. His second return to Assisi certainly brought no glory to the Bernadone name. His dreams were in a shambles and he was puzzled about what to do. He may have been angry with a God who treated him this way. His faith was undergoing a purification. His own dreams were being destroyed to be replaced by a bigger dream that was almost unbelievable.

God's truth often goes against the human grain. To accept God's truth often requires a decision to put our own pet ideas and dreams aside. We become more aware that the Lord wants us and is making us more sensitive to his presence. Rationalizations no longer are satisfactory substitutes for this faith-reality. We begin to recognize the deep-seated

desire within us to be different. We begin to recognize the
call of Someone who is asking for everything. We know that
peace will come only if and when we finally say 'yes' to
that insistent call.

Such a struggle is always deeply personal. It can move us
quickly to our 'yes,' or it may extend itself for days or
months or even years. The people around us influence our
direction. Their belief or lack of it touches our search. Someone who understands can be a pillar of strength in such
moments. But no matter how many real friends touch us in
this struggle, it remains a time of darkness kindled with the
light of hope. We cannot run away from the search. We must
come to grips with ourselves and Jesus. It is a good time,
even when the agony hurts the most.

St Francis lived through such a struggle. He had to face
the doubts in his heart about his way of living. He was
pushed to lonely and weary explorations into the Gospels.
The struggle brought him to prison in Perugia; to emptiness
in partying; to loneliness in sickness; to heartache and misunderstanding. It was a time when Francis had to stretch his
spirit to reach the point of acceptance, freely given. Ever so
slowly, through word and person and event, Francis grew in
awareness that the 'good news' of the gospel is his good
news. He came to know that God did not send his Son
simply to save men in general, but Francis in particular.
Francis came to know that our Father in heaven is not
simply *a* Father, but *my* Father.

Our path shall be similar to this path of Francis. As we
respond to the inner call of Jesus, we discover that Jesus did
not give us a plan of salvation. *He* is the plan of salvation.
The time of that discovery is a very personal thing. But there
are common elements between our search and that of
Francis. Francis became aware slowly. Perhaps it was in the
moments of prayer before the crucifix at San Damiano.
Perhaps as he rode through the silent mountains as the wind
swept through the trees. It may have been in that moment

when he embraced the leper. It may have happened when a
party seemed a bore and his heart longed for more than song
and laughter. Or, it may have been growing through each of
these moments.

At some point he became aware of the love of Jesus. Jesus
came alive for him. As these moments deepened, there was a
more urgent need to respond to Jesus. In this way Francis
came to the point of beginning that was also the end. The
point of deciding to accept the way of Jesus; the point of
deciding to leave behind what was familiar. Now the
Scriptures became important as God's living word to Francis
right now. No longer were they simply a library of books and
dead words linked together. Now the Scriptures were a new
Word, speaking to Francis.

Somehow, in the twilight struggle and the stillness of that
"other," Jesus broke through to the heart of Francis. The
gospels are no longer teachings to listen to, but a person
speaking a word for this moment of my life. No longer can
Francis simply grow in intellectual appreciation of the Truth,
for now there is a relationship with Him who is the Truth. A
commitment to assent to truth is not enough. Now a total
commitment to Jesus is the only way to real life, no matter
what the cost of commitment. Now we can understand the
meaning and implication of those few short words in the
Bishop's court: "I say now . . . our Father who art in
heaven." For now there is no human planning, no marvelous
intellectual structures springing from genius. No, now there is
the handing over of Francis of Assisi into the hands of the
Father to follow the way of Jesus as spelled out in the
gospels. It is now the inner relationship of faith that shall
impel Francis to the adventure of living the gospel life.

> "My life is very monotonous," he (the Fox) said. "I
> hunt chickens and men hunt me. All the chickens are
> just alike, and all the men are just alike. But if you
> tame me, it will be as if the sun came to shine on my

life. I shall know the sound of a step that will be different from all the others. Other steps send me hurrying back underneath the ground. Yours will call me, like music, out of my burrow. And then look, you see the wheat fields down yonder? I do not eat bread. Wheat is of no use to me. The wheat fields have nothing to say to me. And that is sad. But you have hair that is the color of gold. Think how wonderful that will be when you have tamed me! The grain, which is also golden, will bring me back the thought of you. And I shall love to listen to the wind in the wheat . . ."

The Little Prince de St Exupery 83

Francis chose to be 'tamed' by Jesus. His word, his gospel, now called Francis out of his cave and into the sunlight of commitment. And creation brought back to Francis the reminder of the presence of the Father and he loved to 'listen to the wind in the wheat.'

5. Christ Is Alive and Well

WHERE DO I FIND JESUS? People seem to want to discover a sure-fire method for discovering Jesus. It would be good to be able to say that all you have to do is search. That is true. You can't just sit around and wait for something to happen. You do have to seek and knock in order to find and gain entrance to the presence of Jesus. Jesus is always there. The problem is always on our side of the relationship.

An important quality in our search for Jesus is *common sense*. Not the kind of common sense that hides in a corner when the going gets rough nor the common sense that leaves God out of the life that we live. Not the common sense that shouts: "Prudence! Prudence!" when a dash of risk-taking is required.

The quality of common sense we need here is based on some of the faith-elements we have already explored. It includes the ability to face the *whole* of reality and not just bits and pieces of it. It is a willingness to persist in the search even when things seem bleak. It is a readiness for self-discipline that will keep our search properly oriented. It is the ability to allow Jesus to be himself instead of reshaping him into an image pleasing to ourselves. It is the ability to sense the need for reflection and silence in the process of our searching.

But perhaps more importantly, we need to be poor. Poor enough to hope against hope. Poor enough to rely on Jesus when he seems strangely silent. Poor enough to recognize our human limitations. Poor enough to know that there are

37

things we are unable to do alone. Poor enough to receive from Jesus and others the help we need and to recognize our dependence on them. Poor enough to respond to Jesus as well as possible when we are not certain what he wants. Poor enough to take individual, personal action when it would be easier to back off. Poor enough to recognize that we may not have honestly faced the fear that holds us back, that keeps us from being the person we are called to be.

Such poverty will teach us to rely on God in faith. It will bring us to seeing our absolute need of his Spirit to accomplish the goals we are seeking. It will bring us to a faith-maturity that will be ready to accept the Word of God and to respond more and more deeply to the consequences of that Word. It will bring us to take the risk of real love and follow the gospel even when the path seems shrouded in mystery and darkness.

Common sense of this kind is possible for us. It is not easy to achieve, but it is possible. As clouds can blot out the sun, problems sometimes seem to blot out the presence of Jesus. Sometimes the light can be too strong. We cannot see the stars during the daytime because it is too light. So too, our successes sometimes glare too brightly for us to see Jesus in daily life. Yet he is still present just as the stars. So there will be a need to walk in darkness at times so that we can see. Our coming to this 'seeing' will be unique to each of us, but it is a reality. We struggle to become free enough to belong completely to Jesus. There is turmoil within us until we are free enough to trust him. None of us will escape this struggle to grow in faith, hope and love. Each of us wrestles with his own spirit in 'letting loose' of self and being truly poor. St Paul experienced this struggle. He asked Jesus to remove the intensely personal agony it brought him. In answer he was told simply: "My strength is sufficient for you." St Augustine too speaks of this struggle to reach out to Jesus. He speaks of trying again and again and yet drawing back from the very edge of commitment only to be drawn again by the

Lord. So we speak of reality, a reality that cannot be imposed on us from the outside but which must be sought from within. It is that inner struggle of saying 'yes' to everything Jesus wants. It is this cross that we take up day after day. It is this constant search for wholeness that will come only when our 'yes' is so total that there is nothing left to give. Common sense tells us that this struggle, this search cannot be escaped. It can only be delayed or repressed or drowned in the noise of self-seeking.

We will walk this path with Francis. He met this issue with common sense. He did not suddenly come to a moment of conversion nor an emotional high that settled everything. The way to Jesus is much more lonely than that. It has over-tones of Gethsemane that is colored by who and what we are. It may be long or short. That is dependent on God's plan and our response to it. It seems like a paradox. We are asked to say a free 'yes' to a loving plan prepared by our Father. He waits for our free response and will never be content with mere slavish obedience. We are no longer slaves, but friends.

Jesus is alive. He is our friend. He holds back nothing that he can give us. We simply find ourselves unable to have that same, free, total sense of giving in response to Jesus. There are so many detours we can take. We can keep running around doing good and stilling the quiet voice speaking within us. We can sit back and do nothing, discussing things to death in an intellectual gluttony. We can be very adept at avoiding the reality of Jesus so that no demands are made on us, no consequences of real faith have to be accepted. But in all this escaping there is none of the common sense we spoke about. We are neither hot nor cold, but lukewarm, worthy only to be vomited out of his mouth! To ignore Jesus is the cruelest injury and insult of all.

We will be spiritually practical. We can see rightly only with the heart. What is essential is invisible to the eye. Yet how we persist in wanting visual evidence. But how can any one of us package the loneliness within, waiting for someone who cares? What words can convey the feeling of emptiness when we refuse Jesus some corner of life? Who can paint the darkness covering a spirit that hates itself because it sees only the sinful actions that seem to blot out the Son? You and I want proof of the presence of Jesus. But even if it were able to be proven logically, that would not make you his follower. What pleases the mind may simply bore the heart. There is no other way to find Jesus than by letting loose of ourselves. We find him by being poor, or we may never discover him!

In the attic corners of our self, away from our blustering and image-making; away from the desire for applause, we know a deep need for some *One* who can fill our longing and make us whole. We long for someone who will look at us and say: "I love you." Not, "I love you because Jesus says I must love you" nor "I love you because of what I can make of you," nor "I will love you if you will change." We simply want to hear a simple and sincere: "I love you." A transitive verb that links the "I" and the "You" together. A relationship that bonds and ties and tames. A relationship that creates in me the desire to be the best self I can be. A love that will not judge me but will not let me wallow in self-pity. A love whose creative power draws me to heights I had never even thought I could climb. The kind of love that comes from a man-God, hanging on a cross of pain. A man-God who has faced the consequences of love and accepted all of its risks. A man-God who says to you and me: "I love you," with no strings attached.

Francis of Assisi brought another quality to the search for Jesus that is important. In Francis there is a 'stretching' for the truth. Francis prepared himself for such stretching by responding to the truth he already knew. After his break with his father, he walked, singing, in the snow covered forest. But he was not whistling in the dark. He knew his direction even though he was not certain what would happen next. Accepting God as his Father did not mean getting a blueprint for life. The ideas he had in the woods that snowy day were not necessarily in accord with what reality would bring. He did not know everything the Father would ask of him. But neither did he fret about it. His direction was bound to a person, not a plan. He was walking with One who said: "I am the way, the truth and the life." When you walk with Jesus you don't need blueprints.

St Francis recognized two very important truths about himself. 1) I am a sinner. 2) I am called to be a saint. Many people today have no trouble accepting the first. They play the sinner role with gusto. They are often a joyless people whose acceptance of their sinner image makes life a pathway strewn with hidden traps that maim and destroy the spirit. All of us can admit being sinners. But that truth, by itself, does not liberate us. Indeed, it may enslave us. Without the second truth there is little to hope for. Jesus calls us to be saints. We can be more than sinners. We have the possibility of intimacy with Jesus and can grow to wholeness in the relationship. We can break loose of the chains of sinfulness and be someone with Jesus. When we combine these two truths we are in touch with reality. We are sinners and we do need a savior. We are called to be saints and that calls us to hope for an interior growth beyond our wildest imaginings. When we separate these truths we walk in an unreal world. The absolute self-confidence of St Peter before Jesus' passion shows an overabundance of self. "Even though everyone else will deny you, I will never deny you!" Yet it is this same Peter who could not acknowledge being a friend of Jesus when asked by a young woman. After Jesus had risen from the dead, Peter is much wiser. When Jesus asked him: "Do you love me?", Peter replied simply and honestly: "Lord, you know all things; you know that I love you." An answer that recognizes Jesus and confesses to follow the call.

If we are going to have a faith-sense of direction, we too will need to accept Jesus' way of life. It is not very comforting to go it alone. We search for that some one who can make sense of life. Some Germans believed that Hitler could do it for them. Some Russians believe that a Communist State can do it for them. Some people think that a Guru can do it for them. Whoever we may choose to follow, we will need to take a stand with them if we hope to give direction to our lives. It's either commitment to another or we will have to establish our own religion and/or way of life.

Francis asks us to accept the truth as it is proportioned to our present understanding. For us it will mean a prompt response to the Spirit. This Spirit of Jesus called Francis to "repair my Church which is falling to ruin." Francis responded to his understanding of the message at that moment. He became a stone mason and fixed the walls and roof of the physical building. He did not yet understand the full impact of the message. He did act on what he knew. When he left the courtroom of the Bishop, barefoot and poor, he had no special blueprint for living. He only knew a burning desire in his heart to seek God. So he simply tried to respond to God's revelation to him as it came, day by day. For Francis, Jesus is the way and there is no other. Francis walked this way, discovering more and more of the truth as he pilgrimed through the world of his Father.

> A life situation and its light is a gift of God. Each situation is a sacrament in which I meet his revealing presence. He reveals to me what my life should be when I listen in humility and surrender. Consequently, there is never a moment in which I can say: "Now I know exactly what my life will be." A project of existence is not a blueprint, a schedule or a timetable. On the contrary, it is a continually changing awareness of God's will for me. If I see my plan of life as a blueprint, I am liable to become very rigid, very stiff, very difficult to deal with. I may become upset if I find myself in a place or with a duty that I did not foresee in my timetable of life. As a result, I am irritated, angry, rebellious, and

what I really rebel against is life itself . . . Life goes on; new demands are made, and I must go on responding to these demands, no matter how painful, how disillusioning, how disturbing they may be. If I respond generously, I shall develop new aspects of my existence. I shall become a deeper, richer, stronger, more versatile person.

Religion and personality Van Kaam 21

This brings us to a new perspective on the search. We cannot wait until everything is all together before we believe in Jesus. We accept Jesus and move along his way as he reveals himself to us. We reach out to the possibilities of life and see that they lead us to Him who is the way. There is no other way for the Franciscan to go; no other truth to seek; no other life to live than in Jesus. Like Francis, we will take life seriously and we will take Jesus seriously. We will maintain our sense of direction and feel free to laugh at ourselves.

In plenty as well as penury, one had to maintain that sense of direction. One has to keep moving. A flabby mind is unprepared for the full revelation of truth. And earthbound man is bound to earth's stagnation. We need to be quick if we are to be fully quickened by the Spirit. We have to keep going to God if we are to discover that He is the way.

Cord, Sister Mary Francis, September, 1970 276

The way to Jesus requires discipline. When we choose to follow Francis, we will not accept the fly-by-night people who would give us 'instant' religion and quick conversions. Not for the followers of Francis the comfort of painless growth without the cross. Not for us the contentment of being 'saved' and having to do nothing more. Not for us any merely human sensitivity that can be a mask for self-centeredness. Franciscans may not stop at the bottom of the hill called Calvary. We cannot accept emotional 'highs' as substitutes for faith. We are only too well aware that the battle to follow Jesus is not a single combat fought in full view of all. It is a lifetime of seeking and discovery. Once begun, we must do our best never to turn back, never turn away from Jesus if he does not fit our pre-conceived ideas of him.

To follow the gospel way of life is to be on a journey of discovery. It is a journey that is, in its turn, magnificent, frustrating, exhilarating, depressing, satisfying and mystifying. Jesus loves us so much, yet we can so easily run from his love. So often we create our own problems, our own hurts. But, as Jesus said, the seed must die in order to live. An oak tree does not leap from an acorn to a mighty oak. A child, learning to play the piano, is not immediately expected to write sonatas. We have to wait for the oak. We allow the budding musician time to learn. So too, we will need time to learn, but we will never cease traveling. We are pilgrims, a people always arriving and always starting out again. At our head, clear-sighted and fresh-visioned, is a man named Francis. Behind him, through over seven centuries, are people who have chosen to follow this pilgrim on his journey to the dream of following the gospel.

6. To Be a Servant

AMONG THE MANY CRISES that we experience today is the crisis of authority. We may be 'blessed' (?) with an over-abundance of authority. Everyone is becoming an authority. Old people tell young people how to live. Young people tell old people that they ought to think this way or that way. People in between are torn between the two in a confusion about who is correct. It seems that everyone is claiming to know what to do, but despite all that 'authority,' things do not seem to get better.

My assessment may be extreme and a bit simplistic. But I believe that Francis of Assisi has something of importance to say on this point. His common sense approach coupled with his honest response to the gospel gives him a special insight into this vexing problem.

Authority is a necessity. It can be used poorly or wisely. Like anything human, people can use it or abuse it. But even the worst forms of abuse that authority suffered from those who exercised it does not mean that authority ought to be done away with. Francis does not counsel us to destroy authority and start all over again. He simply asks us to apply the principles of the gospels in the exercise of authority.

The 750 plus years that the Franciscan Order has existed has seen many crisis. They often dealt with the concept and the living of the vow of poverty. But many were also concerned with authority. Francis was an essentialist and sought his values in the gospel. When he spoke about the friars who would be superiors in his Order, he always spoke of them as servants, and as those who 'minister' to the brothers. His demands of superiors were based on the words of Jesus who had come to serve and not to be served.

Those who would follow this spirit of Francis are called to the same gospel ideal on authority. Authority will require a sincere and total dedication to the idea of brotherly service. In the Franciscan way of life, the men and women who hold authority are expected to be servants of all the brethren. Jesus is clear on this point. We must learn what it means to be last if we wish to be first. We must choose the lowest place if we would be ready for being called to a higher place. Seeking the first place in things is not in accord with the gospel ideas of Jesus.

Francis recognized this clear imperative of the gospel. He expects those in authority in the Franciscan Order to be especially concerned to give loving service. Even when they must correct or punish, he exhorts them to do it in a manner that will bring the brother to a deeper commitment to Jesus and our way of life. Anger and an overbearing attitude must be avoided. But, on the other hand, Francis charges the brothers who minister in positions of authority to maintain the dedicated spirit so necessary for our way of life. Should any Franciscan refuse to live the gospel, or become a source of diminishing the spirit of the Order, the minister is admonished by Francis to act quickly and promptly for the good of the Brotherhood. Here too we see how demanding a task he asks of superiors. To be the one who ministers to all and yet to be responsible for the growth of the spirit in fraternity life can be a difficult course to chart. Even serving is not always clearly charted.

The superior is to help all the brethren to pray. He is to be especially concerned with the growth in compassion and love within the fraternity. He must build solidly on the rich traditions of our Franciscan heritage, but be ready to move into the unknown ways of the future. He must be receptive to the Spirit and prayerfully attentive to the call of that

Spirit in the fraternity. As 'minister,' he must heal wounds and give courage to those who are fearful of change and conversion. He must walk with the weak in tender understanding and challenge the strong to deepened understanding of the weaker brethren.

The superior must be loyal to the Church. Francis was able to avoid becoming another 'splinter' group by clinging to the Church of Jesus. This too is a place of risk. Our love for the Church is not some blind, unthinking acceptance, but a loving, considered and realistic acceptance of the Church as Jesus' presence in today's world. She too can make mistakes in the ways and means she may use. Franciscans will not simply overlook her failing, but work to correct it. Such loyalty can be most difficult. Yet Francis calls us to listen to our Mother, the Church. Superiors must give special witness to that loyalty.

What may be more demanding of anyone who ministers is to be gentle with all. Our fraternity life is not free of disagreement. Franciscans too get angry with one another, even bitter with one another. We too find it difficult to forgive those whose words or actions tear us down. It can be especially difficult to reach out in forgiveness and to be rejected. It is just as easy for a Franciscan to throw in the towel in such a situation as it is for anyone else. Yet, as a Franciscan, we are called to continue to be present to those who are hurting as well as those who hurt us. Superiors can often experience an agony in trying to decide on the way to reconciliation. Yet, here is perhaps the place where intimacy with Christ will grow in the superior. Jesus calls him to absolute dependence in many such situations. He must respond with love to Jesus and with compassion for those who hurt. Even when it is his sad duty to ask a brother to leave for the sake of the fraternity, there is never any joy in this. Even more, he will still want to reach out in whatever way he can to the erring brother or sister.

These consequences of the gospel are a normal thing for one who understands his Franciscan calling. The depth of love or the height of such demands of forgiveness bring us to Jesus. This gospel calling is not for the weak hearted or those who are afraid to love. The lay Franciscans who serve in a position of authority shall soon discover the kind of strength they need in order to minister in love. To serve is a responsibility. But it is also an opportunity to share one's self, one's life, one's time and oftentime one's own emotions and feelings on the deepest level of gift giving. It is another expression of the 'yes' to Christ.

FRANCISCAN STRUCTURE

The growth of the Franciscan movement brought with it the necessity for some form of structure. Without some degree of organization, a movement easily dissolves into a crowd with everyone going his own way. Good structures can avoid such dissipation of the dream and ideals of a founder.

The Franciscan way of life is meant to create an atmosphere (spirit) and environment (structure) in which Franciscans can grow. Spirit and structure must work together. But of the two, it is the spirit that must dominate. Structure must serve the spirit; make it grow; give it assistance in maintaining communication, discipline, unity and sound development. So long as the structure does all of this it is good. It is meant to build up the growth of the spirit of Francis in fraternity life. Structure must never replace spirit nor can organization become more important than spiritual blossoming of Franciscans. In today's world we are changing many things in the 'structure' of the Franciscan way of life. But every change must keep in mind the spirit of Francis and serve to develop that spirit.

So we must test everything in order to know what to keep and what to discard. Testing is always a challenge. To some it can seem to be a threat. It is essential to leave behind the things that no longer serve fraternity life and spirit. But we cannot always find immediate ways to improve things. Often we shall feel that we are walking in darkness as we seek new ways to give life to the spirit of Francis in today's world. But we dare not retreat from the challenge. We will maintain confidence without over-simplification; develop a cautious criticism without biting skepticism; seek gospel ways of acting and not be overwhelmed by business principles. Above all, change will require us to pray always and to keep an open heart; open to the future and open to the richness of the past.

In all of this talk about change, we must never lose sight of what it is we seek. We seek to have a deeper union with Jesus and, through him, with the Father under the powerful influence of the Holy Spirit. We will need to take care not to get caught up in the ways and means and forget the goal. Techniques, methods, new forms of worship, format for meetings, dialogue and discussion are all means. It is vital that we do not make them more important than our goal. They are meant to help us come to union with Jesus. Intimacy with the risen, human Jesus is what we seek. We must judge our ways and means to see that they help us to that goal. Moreover, different people will have different needs. We will be open to a pluriformity in our ways and means to meet these differing needs. Otherwise we can easily become a narrow, boxed-in fraternity, having little resemblance to the Spirit-filled community established by St Francis.

Once again we can see some of the consequences of our Franciscan commitment. It will require openness both to the Spirit and to our brothers and sisters. It may require letting loose of pet ideas and ways of doing things. It may ask of us that we change patterns of living that interfere with fraternity growth. But it is our way to the Father. We shall not turn back nor refuse to work at developing a vibrant fraternity for all.

So, Father, give me a clear mind and an open heart so that I may do your work and not my own. Help me to be concerned and compassionate with others rather than trying to keep things comfortable for myself. I ask this of you, Father, in the name of Jesus your Son and my Brother, and in the name of St Francis who served you so well. Amen

7. Going My Way

TODAY WHEN WORDS LIKE 'LIFESTYLE' and 'doing your own thing' and 'encounter groups' and similar words and ideas are normal topics of conversation, we would like to explore a few ideas about the lifestyle of a Franciscan. If we want to follow Francis we will need to look at his approach to living the gospels.

There is a general umbrella that we use to cover everything connected with Jesus. It is the name 'Christian.' That name covers a multitude of lifestyles that sometimes seem at odds with one another. The 'Jesus people' certainly consider themselves to be Christians. People living in communes consider themselves to be Christians. People who are fundamentalist and literal in their interpretation of Scripture call themselves Christians. Groups of people who take a weekend 'walk with Christ' come away as Christians. Gentle people working to respond to the whole gospel call themselves Christians. The term 'Christian' certainly covers a wide spectrum of belief and practice. Though it may appear that it makes us all one, the reality does not always bear this out. There are some Christians who leave out any consideration of the suffering Christ in their lifestyle. Only the risen Christ is talked about. Others preach a doomsday gospel, an 'end of the world' gospel of fear. Some Christians condemn everyone who believes differently than themselves. Others narrow the gospel to fit pre-conceived notions that fit comfortably in their lives. This word 'Christian' suffers from over-use and has lost some of its real meaning in the process.

The lifestyle of Francis is based on trying to live the whole gospel just as it is.

> This is the rule and life of the 'Little Brothers' . . . namely, to observe the Gospel of our Lord Jesus Christ.
> *Rule of the First Order* St Francis

At the end of his life, Francis wrote his own brief commentary on his way of life in his last will and testament. He wrote:

> And after the Lord gave me some brothers, there was nobody to show me what to do; but the most High Himself revealed to me that I was to live according to the form of the Holy Gospel. And I caused it to be written down in few and simple words.

If then, we were to list some of the fundamental values of our Franciscan way of life, the following would certainly be important.

1) Franciscans are to take the whole gospel seriously.

2) Our following of the gospel is subject to the approval and continuing support of the Church.

3) Franciscans must develop, in a practical way, the attitudes and values, the ways of acting and approach to life that we find in the gospel of Jesus Christ.

4) Franciscans are expected to develop an openness to discovery and conversion that will call for constant growth and deeper response to the gospel as our personal way of life.

5) Franciscans commit themselves to an on-going process of growing in intimacy with Jesus through their profession of the Franciscan way of life.

6) Franciscans become more and more aware that it is the Spirit of Jesus who shall make us holy. Without Him we can do nothing, but with Him all things are possible. We are poor alone, but rich in Christ Jesus, our Lord.

The gospel way of life is filled with limitless opportunities for growth. We will never grow stagnant if we are open to the Spirit speaking through the Scriptures. When we get to feeling smug about things, the Word of God shakes us loose and moves us to new discoveries and more generous response. It becomes obvious that our way of life will require consistency in reflecting on the Word of God and incorporating our conclusions into everyday life. Persistence in gospel living will require a more and more intense response to Jesus' word. Until the day we die, we shall be stretching our spirit and seeking new horizons for living. We will need discipline. The gospel life is not a rose-covered path leading to Glories Ltd. Here is the way one Franciscan describes it:

> Notwithstanding, all the justified criticism in the world will ever really remove the basic fact of our need for constant vigilance, for self-control, for victory over our own hearts. "If a man wishes to come after me, he must deny his very self, take up his cross, and begin to follow in my footsteps." The debunking of asceticism now in vogue is just another form of death-dealing naivete.

> We must not forget that asceticism is not sanctity, is not our goal, is not life with God. It is only a means to the end. But it is a necessary means, especially in our present set-up. Without its prudent but forceful application, no life with God could ever survive in our heart.
> *Our life with God*, Koser OFM 38

If we wish to follow the gospel life discipline and self-denial will be required. The form that such self-denial takes will need to be tailored to our individual needs. But it will be essential to our journey.

Since our lifestyle is the gospel, that is the source book for the Franciscan. We cannot dare to explore the whole

gospel in one short chapter. But our Lord has given us a
summary of his way of life in the Sermon on the Mount
where he shared the fundamentals of his message with us. So
we shall share some reflections on the Beatitudes as the core
of the message of Jesus. Our Franciscan calling is special and
Francis wants us to clearly understand that.

> My Brothers, my brothers! God has called me along a
> path of humility and simplicity. I want you not to
> name me any Rule, whether of St Augustine nor of St
> Bernard, nor of St Benedict.

> The Lord said I was to be a new kind of fool in the
> world, and God did not want to lead me along any
> other road but by that knowledge.
>
> *Words of St Francis,* #257

Francis was not a Scripture scholar nor did intellectual
arguments move him very much. His response to the gospels
came from a heart of faith and not a head full of facts. We
can follow such a man, for we too are ordinary people who
can learn to care and love and follow the man with a heart
for all people. Francis was people-centered. He enjoyed
people and cared about them. The beggar who asked alms of
him in his father's store knew this care. The friar who was
hungry and needed Francis' companionship at his meal
received what he sought. If Francis is a new kind of fool, it is
the kind of 'foolery' we are all capable of following.

When the people-centered Francis of the 13th century
comes in touch with the people-centered Jesus of the 1st
century, a real blending occurs. Francis is absorbed by Jesus.
He leaves everything to follow Jesus. Francis does not
indulge in long philosophical discussions about following
Jesus. He simply reacts spontaneously and naturally to the
call of his Jewish friend. Francis experienced a long struggle
to come to the point of commitment. But once he made his

decision, it was a wholehearted and total one.

When our Father calls us to follow Francis, we too will struggle to come to the point of total commitment. Our organizational abilities may lag behind the dynamics of modern times; our structural setup may not match the corporate image-making some groups project. But we must always be people-centered and a people of faith. Jesus must be at the heart and soul of our life. We must be a 'new kind of fool' in our time. We are treading on risky soil here. Falling in love with Jesus will lead to all kinds of unknown and unexpected paths. It can be risky and it sometimes seems frightening. If we want to be comfortable, than the Franciscan way of life is out. When we choose to go this way, then we will accept not only the initial 'yes,' but also accept every single consequence of that 'yes' as it comes to us.

To follow the Franciscan way of life and to be a fool for Jesus can sound romantic. But the reality requires more than romantic dreams and mushy words of love. This is a serious decision to make. We are not called thus by God in order to toy with the call. Our Father will constantly ask for more from us. We shall be his friends, the recipients of his innermost secrets. We shall be responsible for sharing his riches through our life. We shall be persecuted if we really believe and live our belief, because the student is not greater than the Master. We shall endure the pain of crucifixion, perhaps betrayal, for this is the pattern of Jesus. Being a fool for Christ will not be altogether glamorous. But it will bring real peace and joy and wholeness. Jesus has promised that, and he is true to his promise. But the price will be life itself: "Whoever loses his life for my sake will find it."

Francis of Assisi was a poet. He was thoughtful and aware of life. He could come alive like sparkling fireworks or be quiet as the winds wandering through the pines on a mountainside. His conversion was not instant nor magic nor easy. He puzzled over it. He prayed over it. He walked in darkness seeking it. Everything that had meant 'security' now meant nothing to him. But there seemed to be no replacement for the loss. Life became a burden instead of a joy as he pilgrimed to the point of total acceptance of Jesus. He knew something must be done. He was not certain what it would be. He knew the Lord was calling but where? What does He want? How do I follow him?

Stones. His first response to Jesus' words from the San Damiano Crucifix is to collect stones. Stones to repair the old church building. He begged stones from old friends and relatives. He became a fool in their eyes. His break with his father was dramatic and final, but he was still seen as a fool. There is a deep risk in becoming a fool for Christ. Perhaps he was misreading God's message. But the time for procrastination and indecision was over. This shall be the way for Francis!

You may find yourself in this same situation. You feel you might want to follow the Franciscan way of life. But you are not certain. It is obvious by now that it will not be an instant moment to holiness. You will not be relieved of the struggle with yourself as you try to let loose of the things that keep you from Jesus. Neither can you pick and choose bits and pieces from the gospel that suit your fancy. You will need to take it all, plainly, simply and without mutilation or manipulation. You will be faced with all the consequences of such a choice. A lot of dying to selfishness will be required if you follow the whole gospel. Many of your pet excuses and rationalizations will have to bite the dust. "Our Father, who art in heaven" will have to be more than words.

The Franciscan way of life is not child's play. It is not a child's slide to holiness. It is more like climbing a mountain, tough and demanding. But it will also be full of surprises in the views we discover together as we climb higher. We will discover, as we climb, a view that was unthinkable in the valley of comfort and ease. This way of life ought to shake you. New insights and honest response to the gospel of Jesus will bring wider perspectives to life. No longer will you be able to rest on past accomplishments. Always there will be the call to stretch out your spirit to the needs of this present moment. If you respond to the reality of your call to follow Francis, your life will not be the same.

Jesus gave us his fundamental message in the Beatitudes. It is a clear outline of what we are called to be. We want to reflect on the meaning of the Sermon on the Mount and implement them in our personal lives. Since they are so essential to the gospel message, they will be essential to our Franciscan way of life.

Many Scripture scholars believe that the gospel-writers put together in the Sermon on the Mount the fundamental beliefs of Jesus. They feel that it was meant to be a sort of summation of his message of salvation. More important, the Beatitudes are not meant to talk simply of rewards we will receive in heaven. Quite the contrary. They offer blessings for right now! They are a challenge to us to embrace the whole of Jesus' message so that we might receive the promises. It takes a heap of living to make them come alive in our lives. But living is what we are all about. Reflect on these words and plant them in the soil of your life. They are the heart of the message of Jesus.

Blessed are you poor, for yours is the kingdom of heaven. The key word in this statement is the word "poor." The word that is used in the original text is "Anawim." In the Bible Anawim is used to describe those who were disadvantaged and downtrodden; a people who had lost everything except hope. In the midst of the most devastating physical and emotional and spiritual suffering, the Anawim clung to God in faith and hope. When there was no human reason to believe, they believed! When human frustration and helplessness filled their lives, they were loyal to God and believed in his promises. They were a little people who would not allow human events to turn them from God. These Anawim were the 'poor ones' to whom the good news would first be preached. They were to be specially blessed by God.

They would be the first to receive the message of the coming of the kingdom of God.

The Anawim are the model for Francis' concept of poverty. He accepted the idea of being a people without human resources who would still believe in Jesus. Francis was willing to accept the idea of being able to do nothing without Christ. He would believe in Jesus when things seemed impossible, because he believed in the promise that 'with God all things are possible.' To Francis, poverty couldn't be isolated from his faith-relationship to Jesus. Being poor was not simply an economic problem. It goes much deeper into the heart of man than that. The economics of gospel poverty are a consequence of being Anawim and not the cause. Francis sought to be free of being possessed by anything. Whatever might be clung to could be a tie that kept him from the freedom of the gospel. It could be a pet idea or a pattern of action. It could be a material possession or an attitude of mind. Anything at all that kept his 'yes' from being complete was an obstacle to real poverty. Becoming poor was to accept a lifetime of enlarging his 'yes' to the Lord. He wrote this way about Lady Poverty:

> There are many people who devote themselves to prayers and devotions, and practice bodily restrictions and afflictions of many kinds, but at a single word that seems offensive to their person, or at anything taken away from them, they are quickly scandalized and upset.
>
> Such people are not truly poor in spirit, because anyone who is truly poor in spirit hates himself and loves those who slap him in the face.
>
> *Words of St Francis*, #191m

Our Franciscan calling requires a constant handing over of our self to Jesus. It means openness to the Lord's work no

matter what dispossessing that may require. It is understanding that Francis meant every word when he prayed so
simply: "My God and my all."

*Oh, the happiness of those who mourn, for they shall be
comforted.* This beatitude speaks to those who are broken
hearted and sad. But it is not simply a personal loss that is
involved here. It has a wider meaning. This mourning is not
only for a friend who has died or who is in trouble. It is
sorrow over the sad state to which God's people have fallen
through unfaithfulness and sin. It is pain experienced by a
people whose relationship with God has been shaken and
shattered by sin. So very often the Psalmist speaks in these
terms, crying out to Yahweh in the name of all his people.
The comfort that is promised to those who mourn is the
presence of a person who can transform sorrow into joy. The
sorrow springs not only from a personal feeling of being
unfaithful, but from a sense of sorrow for the events that
threaten to overrun God's people. Personal infidelity is seen
as a contributing cause in this national problem. There is a
deep, inner sorrow (mourning) for this infidelity. But there
is also hope and consolation, for God is present to give hope
and consolation.

St Francis experienced this kind of 'mourning' as he
perceived the sorry state of the Church in his day. He was
deeply saddened by the lives of so many who ignored God.
War, anger, hatred had been so much a part of the lives of his
fellowmen. Oppression burdened them with its injustice and
impersonalism. He saw friendships shattered in man's struggle
for power. He saw the clamoring and cheating that was part
of the hunt for wealth and profit. He mourned this non-
sensical turning from God. So he sought to share with people
the gospel that could turn things around. He became God's
instrument in bringing consolation to a people in mourning.

*Blessed are the gentle, the disciplined of heart, they shall
inherit the land.* Some translations use the word 'meek'
instead of 'gentle.' That word makes it sound too much like

being a doormat for everyone. This distorts the real meaning of the beatitude. Jesus is speaking of the person who knows how to handle his emotions and reactions. The reactions of the gentle person is proportioned to the reality of the situation at hand. Whatever is called for by the situation is done. It may be gentle compassion or righteous anger. But the person who is 'disciplined' of heart will face the situation with gospel realism. Such a person is going to be in 'possession' of the situation. The term 'inheriting the land' is a symbol of having this kind of 'possessing' of the situation. It is the spiritual blessing of knowing what life is all about according to the faith-perspective of the gospel.

Francis learned to live this beatitude. He learned to respond to the situations of his life with realism and discipline. He could be angry and firm with dumb and lazy people. He could bend over backwards in kindness to the weak. His response was proportioned to the situation. As he grew in his understanding of the gospel, the patterns of his reactions followed Jesus more and more. He was not afraid to be a gospel-person, for the gospel was his way of life. To be Francis was to be one who lived the gospel. Living this beatitude calls for a great deal of flexibility and willingness to understand others. The stiff and fearful person will find this beatitude difficult to follow. The poor person will find it a natural consequence of being poor.

Oh, the blessedness of those who hunger and thirst for justice, for they shall find satisfaction. This beatitude is subject to two interpretations (at least). In Luke's gospel, it seems that our Lord is speaking about actual, physical hunger. In the gospel of Matthew the hunger seems to reflect a more spiritual meaning. In either case there is a real hunger and thirst involved, and its object is justice. On the one hand we might understand it as meaning the individual's own search for personal, ethical goodness and excellence. In this sense we might read the beatitude this way: "Blessed is the man who hungers for his own ethical improvement." "Blessed

is the man who hungers for moral excellence in his life."
Because he seeks it he will find it.

Another way of looking at this beatitude is to see it as
God's operation in our lives. God has established right as
right and wrong as wrong. He is pleased with those who do
the right and shows his displeasure with those who do wrong.
When you hunger for God's will in your life, and you pray
intensely that things will be set right, God will give you what
you seek. The justice and goodness of God will prevail.

The fundamental concept involved here is the fact that
you will be blessed if you persist in seeking the will of God,
in sanctifying his name and in a growing awareness of the
work of the Spirit in your life. Jesus is blessing conformity
to and understanding of the will of the Father and consistent
efforts to implement it. Blessed are you if you assume
responsibility for glorifying God's name.

Francis hungered to do the will of the Father. He thirsted
to implement the Father's will in his life. Till the moment
when Sister Death called him home, Francis had a deep
hunger and thirst to discover and respond to the will of the
Father. Francis responded to that will as he understood it at
any given moment. Responsiveness led to deepened understanding and a stronger and more wholehearted response. It
brought him the fulfillment and wholeness that comes with
accepting the will of the Father. Like Francis, we are called
to hunger and thirst for the will of the Father. We too will
discover it gradually and each new response will make us
more sensitive to that will of the Father.

*Blessed are those who are merciful, for they shall find
mercy.* In one word this beatitude speaks of 'compassion.'
In the Old Testament God is often described as a God of
compassion. He reaches out again and again to his people,
even when they are not faithful. He always gives another
chance. Mercy, compassion and loving-kindness are characteristic of God. Mercy is the willingness to go out on a
limb for another. It means much more than simply not

judging. It is the inner readiness to reach out even when a friend has betrayed your trust. God, our Father, is like that, willing to sacrifice, to risk everything in our behalf. Compassion, feeling with another, is what we see in Jesus. If we show this mercy and compassion, we will receive it in turn from the Father.

This quality of compassion was precious to Francis. In his Rule he reminded the friars to deal with each other as a mother deals with her children. "For if a mother loves her child in the flesh, how much more ought we to love those who are our brothers in the Spirit." His work with the lepers, the outcasts of his society, sprang from his compassionate heart. The life of Francis is filled with actions of compassion and mercy. Francis "feels with" people and responds to inner needs as well as external needs. It is the quality of real compassion that will keep our charity from being a mere 'hand-out' and become an outreach from the heart. Compassion respects another and gives a feeling of worth. We Franciscans ought to be noted for this sort of thing.

Blessed are the pure of heart for they shall see God. To be pure of heart means moving away from external, formal, ritualistic 'law and order' conformity to Law and embracing an interior, clear-sighted and warm-hearted response to the man-God, Jesus Christ. Jesus is speaking to people who had been overburdened by a 'law-mentality' that imposed external burdens as the only way to goodness. So many minutiae had been added to the Law that an ordinary man simply couldn't keep it. The ordinary man was looked down on by his legal, Pharisaical neighbor. Jesus wants to break this stranglehold of law and mere externals. It is what goes on in the heart that really counts. It is not what men see you doing that makes you good, but what the Father sees within your heart. The Pharisees had imposed regulation after regulation, some 613 in all. It became impossible to even remember all of them, much less to obey them. It was an impossible burden. The yoke of Jesus was light because it did not depend on a mechanical, external, rigid conformity. If your heart is right (Pure of heart), the rest will follow. If your heart is filled with an internal moral sensitivity your actions will follow suit. If your internal values are in good order and you live by them, you will be able to see God in life. You will 'see' him through an internal experience of his presence. Blessed are the pure in heart who practice this clear-sighted, morally sensitive way of life. They will experience God by love and not by legalism.

Francis described this beatitude in this way:

> They are pure of heart who disregard what the world offers and seek what heaven offers, never ceasing to adore and contemplate the true and living Lord God with a clean heart and mind.
>
> *Words of St Francis*, #191o

In the gospel way of life we must always be certain that law and organization serve the Spirit. We need to have a clear-sighted awareness of God, a sense of contemplation. Scraping away selfishness and self-centeredness, we shall be able to see clearly the will of our Father and experience his presence in our lives.

Blessed are the peacemakers, they shall be called sons of God. Blessed are those who break down barriers, who practice 'shalom.' The word 'shalom' means wholeness and integrity and perfection. To wish 'shalom' to another is to ask God to give him everything he needs to be whole and complete and full of joy. It says that you are willing to help achieve that sort of wholeness for him. It is the finest peace that one can bring. Such a peace allows a person to accept any risk in following Jesus. We can risk failure or rejection, success or joy, for within the innermost recesses of our self we are at peace. Such peace no one can take away for it is based on the creative love of the Father and on the presence of the Spirit. It moves us from self-centeredness to an outreach to God in prayerfulness and to others in love.

What a difference between shalom and what we call peace in our day. Cold-war co-existence is labeled as peace. The cessation of killing is called peace. The suppression by force of violence is called peace. The balance of power among nuclear nations is called peace. Keeping 'law and order' is called peace. On a personal level, silent warfare is called peace so long as nothing is done. Avoiding people we can't stand is called peace. Not getting involved is called peace. How far all of this is from the peace of shalom.

Francis worked for shalom. He longed for wholeness in those he loved. He worked and prayed to bring it about. No effort was too much; no pain too great if it brought shalom. This spirit of Francis must be ours. We will not work for the simple absence of grumbling and conflict in fraternity life. We will seek shalom for all. We will commit ourselves to that no matter what the price. It will be much more than the words of a resolution. It will require deep and loving commitment to fraternity and to the people who are part of fraternity.

> How truly it has been said that community life, community spirit are learned by osmosis. We do not teach love and unity, we COMMUNicate them. We establish them as an atmosphere. We preach them by our attitude without noise of words.
>
> *Marginals*, Sister Mary Francis 89

Every Christian is called to create shalom. For Franciscans it is a special calling. Every effort, every kind of discipline of heart, every manner of forgiveness, every imaginable pain must be accepted to achieve shalom. Anyone who believes that this work is ever finished does not know people too well. Fraternity life will always call for building shalom and therefore for constant renewal. As followers of Francis we must be peace-makers who are at peace with God, within ourselves, with others and with creation. Such an ideal will be the work of a lifetime. But the God who calls us to shalom, will be with us to make it possible.

Oh, the bliss of the martyr's pain, for theirs is the kingdom of heaven. The original meaning of martyr is 'one who gives witness.' In this beatitude it reflects a willingness to give witness to Jesus and his gospel even if it leaves us open to persecution and/or death. This means more than having debates on religion. It means a living witness to the faith in word and in deed, in attitude and commitment. It requires that we take the gospel seriously and not allow persecution to turn us from our chosen path. It is not a game, a playing at being religious. It is living the gospel all the time, everywhere, with everyone, no matter what the price. It means selling everything to buy the pearl of great price.

Francis gave witness to this sort of commitment. His conversion brought him to accept Jesus completely. Nothing was too risky, nothing too demanding if the Lord required it. God called him to be a special kind of fool. If it brought mockery or insult, he refused to turn away from such a special calling.

We are called to that same special way of life, seeking Jesus in the Franciscan way of life. We must follow that gospel way. There is mystery in the call. Why we should be called this way is God's business. When we know the 'call' it is our business to follow it. We are called to give witness to the gospel. It is a privilege to be so loved by God, but it is also a demanding responsibility. If we are true to this calling, if the beatitudes take root in us, they may well lead us to persecution: The downgrading of our calling; the snide remarks about our 'religious fanaticism'; friends not understanding our commitment; our own deepened sensitiveness that makes the hurts more painful. We are called to be a 'beatitude people' and that may not always be easy. But when the Lord calls, we are able to do all this because his power will work in us. In littleness we come to know that it is no longer I who lives, but Christ lives in me!

The beatitudes offer us a path of God's expectations for us. We Franciscans are called to be 'special signs' of the beatitudes in the world. There is no simple, easy, overnight way to achieve such a goal. It will take a persistent, personal, supportive effort of each of us. It will take too an awareness that we walk in fraternity to this goal.

Many serious struggles will face us on this way to life. The conflicts that are part of human living will also be ours. We will have to move beyond 'getting even' or 'pouting' to a real seeking for shalom and reconciliation. Time and effort will be asked of us when we feel we have no time or effort to give. We will be surprised in beautiful moments of joyful sharing as well as hurt by unexpected misunderstanding in people we love. We will be tempted to let down on our efforts and to drift with the stream only to be called to renewal when we seem least able to respond. All along the way Jesus will call for self-giving and generosity and deepen our sense of joy.

It will require clear-sightedness, compassion, forgiveness, poverty and the embrace of the Father's will. But Jesus is present and he shall help us fulfill our calling to be Franciscans.

For the whole of his life, short as it was, Francis was alive! He appreciated in full measure both water and wine; fasting and the almond cookies he requested in his dying hours. He loved life and lived it fully. He founded a great Order and made human blunders. He was capable of ecstacy and vexation. He blessed some of his followers and cursed others who, he said, "pulled down what he and the others built up!" He never had the inglorious achievement of not having blundered because he hadn't tried. Francis could have been as great a sinner as he was a saint, but he could never have been a half-way sinner any more than he was a half-way saint. Being half-alive was not for him. He was not afraid of greatness but it came to him through seeking to be poor. The call of the Father was not too big for Francis, for he walked with Jesus, his brother. Even pain could not hinder him from the journey for he embraced it with a love that carried him to new heights.

> It is not sorrows which deplete us so much as sorrow half-accepted. The cross is salvific only when it is carried, not when it is grudgingly dragged along.
>
> *Cord* December, 1970, 374

When we embrace the Franciscan way of life, it becomes *our* way of life. Other involvements and organizations may be important, but this calling must always take priority. Our call to follow the Franciscan way of life will lead to a deeper and more sensitive acceptance of family responsibility, social responsibility, parish responsibility, prayer responsibility. It is a call to follow Jesus in everything that he asks of us. Our mere human love is enhanced and expanded as it is blended with the love of Jesus. In our struggle to put first things first, we shall seek wisdom and understanding from the Lord. Standing still before our Lord, we shall be quiet enough to hear his voice.

> In the name of the encouragement you owe me in Christ, in the name of the solace that love can give, of fellowship in spirit, compassion and pity, I beg you; make my joy complete by your unanimity, possessing the one love, united in spirit and ideals, Never act out of rivalry or conceit, rather, let all parties think humbly of others as superior to themselves, each of you looking to others' interests rather than your own.
>
> Philippians 2: 1 - 4

8. Getting Together

IN THE SHORT SPAN OF 44 YEARS, Francis of Assisi initiated a movement-community that helped to change society. He preached his message of Lady Poverty to a people in love with luxury. To people saturated with years of war and intra-city fighting, he preached peace. To a people who were sad and depressed and on the fringes of society's life, he preached about the joy that comes in following the gospel. He was different and unique, and he made an impact because he was himself.

There was something of God's own special kind of dealing with men in Francis' gentle way of communication. When everyone else was coveting more and more power and property, Francis asked for nothing. To a society that was caught up in the struggle to achieve prominence, he preached the value of littleness. Unlike many who call themselves religious, he did not 'use' poverty to get what he wanted or try to hide behind a smokescreen of rightness and respectability. On the contrary, he was quite delighted to be considered a fool. It is rather difficult to know what to do with such a person. Every punishment or put-down became another means for him to rise to his Lord. The men and women who came in touch with Francis could not really get him out of their lives again. The same force that called Jesus to bear witness to the will of his Father was now at work in the hills around Assisi.

Francis attracted many followers in the aftermath of his conversion. His joy and ability to reach out to others was an attractive thing to follow. It is refreshing to hear God praised and to have someone honestly consider you to be a worthy person. Francis felt that if God was able to change Francis of Assisi, he would have little trouble with the people Francis met. By the time that Sister Death ended his life, Francis had thousands of followers.

The attraction of Francis brought many to follow him. But not all of them had the same, single-minded dedication to the gospel way of life. Many among them were the 'instant conversion' people who quickly burned out in the face of suffering. Others refused to walk in the 'little way' and sought power and prestige in the Order of Francis. Francis suffered much because of so many friars who did not understand his dream. They dulled it with mediocrity and hazed it over with legalisms and rationalizations. In his frustration, Francis cried out: "Too many friars minor! Would that the world might marvel at their fewness!" The followers of Francis faced the perennial problem of all groups in all ages. As numbers increased, fervor decreased. Franciscans constantly faced the problem of keeping the vision and spirit of Francis alive in the heart of the community dedicated to his way of life.

Like the question posed in the musical "Fiddler on the Roof," we too might ask: "If it's so dangerous, why do you stay up there?" Why persist in the struggle to build community life if it is so much work and hassle? Why not simply let everybody do what they want and find Jesus on their own? The answer is simple. We do it because the dream of Francis must not die. His vision of fraternal brotherhood must continue for it expresses the community the gospels call for. It must live in every age and at every time so that it can be available to all who are called. Most of all, this community is rich with opportunities for our time. We cannot discard the riches God offers us through the Franciscan way of life.

The model for the Christian community is the Trinity. In

the Trinity we have three distinct persons bound together in one nature so that there is one God and not three. The Trinity is a community of Father, Son and Holy Spirit caught up in the constant action of a burning love and knowledge of one another that delights and satisfies. It is a bond of love so intense and a knowing that is so complete that unity is a natural and normal consequence. It is three distinct persons acting as one without losing their distinctness. When Jesus spoke about this unity he could only ask that his followers be as close as is the Trinity.

> I pray for those who will believe in me through their word, that all may be one as you, Father, are in me, and I in you; I pray that they may be one in us, that the world may believe that you sent me.
>
> John 17: 21

Our witness to the world is tied to the sign of our unity with one another and with the Father so that 'the world may believe that you sent me.' This vision of Christ is the vision of Francis too.

Jesus' personal unity with the Father is something very special in him. Throughout his life, he reiterated again and again the theme that his Father's will was everything for him. There was such a deep identification between the human Jesus and the Father that Jesus could not be himself apart from the Father. Even in the agonizing test of death it was so. Even though the Father seemed not to hear; though Jesus cried out: "My God, why have you abandoned me!" he still handed over his spirit to this same Father. Separation from the Father would be worse than death or abandonment. This is the dedication and identification that Francis of Assisi embraced. No matter what suffering would be required; no matter how many betrayals of the dream might arise, Francis would stay on this way. Our feeling for developing fraternity-community is not based on sentimental togetherness nor merely on emotion. Rather it must be a strong, vibrant, eager love that walks through the valley of pain or the mountains of joy with equal responsiveness. Even when God himself seems silent, this brand of love will still cling to the will of the Father.

A gospel-community will be a community that can suffer for Jesus. A gospel-community will offer itself, even to death, for those it loves. A gospel-community never turns in on itself in selfish exclusiveness yet never forgets to cherish those who share the dream. A gospel-community maintains a constant, consistent, compassionate, joyful readiness to respond to life. It can never become a spiritual snob-unit without losing its heart. A gospel-community recognizes its failures and works to correct them. It knows how constant is the need for renewal and conversion. A gospel-community expends every effort to create an atmosphere of warmth and acceptance that allows all members to grow in Christ. It must recognize the absolute necessity for prayer and prayerfulness. Community unity is based on unity with Jesus. No mere activity can ever supplant prayer in knowing the Lord. Neither shall we substitute finding Christ in people for discovering the Lord through a personal, prayerful relationship.

> Insofar as the passage (from Ezechiel 3:18) must be applied generally, I take it to mean that the servant of God ought to be so aflame in his personal life and holiness as to reprove all the wicked by the light of his example and the tongue of his association with others. In that way, I say, the luster of his life and the fragrance of his good name will denounce their wickedness to everybody.
>
> *Words of St Francis*, #225

This process of growing in Christ never ends. A true gospel-community never ceases to stretch its spirit to apply the gospel message. The men and women who follow Francis are called to help continue this process in fraternity life. We look forward to what lies ahead, straining to the goal laid out for us by Christ.

The term 'community' is loosely applied to many kinds of groups. We might understand our own ideas of gospel community by examining some of these groups.

Groups of people who gather together to accomplish social changes and goals are often called communities. Such groups are often work-oriented. They set out to change structures or institutions, situations and patterns of behavior in order to promote peace or justice or similar goals. Such goals can keep the group together for a long time. When work-goals are achieved, the 'community' tends to disband unless it finds another work goal. Take note of the vast change in the Union movement from its beginning to now. Notice how many protest groups disband when goals are reached or even seen as unreal and unreachable. While such groups exist, they are often termed community-action groups. This use of the word 'community' does not coincide with the gospel-community ideal.

In the Church we call parishes 'local communities.' They truly ought to be that. But often the parish community is not the gospel-community it is called to be. Many parishes have 1000 families or more. Every Saturday and Sunday there are five, six or more Masses to accommodate the people. Confessions are heard at particular times. Various special programs go on, CCD, CFM, CYO, Women's societies and societies for men. Despite this organization, most people find themselves at Mass on Sunday among people they do not know. Those they do know are often known through non-parochial contacts. There is little in the way of inter-action at Mass. Relationships often grow through other contacts, the barber or hairdresser, local store owner, garage mechanic, friends with kids in the same grades in school, other members of the Senior Citizens group. If it were not for Sunday Mass, you simply would never even see many of the people of the parish-community. There are always the 'regulars' in every parish who know each other because they are the work-force in the parish. But the average parishioner is not a regular. For many reasons, then, many parishes cannot be considered to be communities.

Another grouping-together of people happens when people of mutual interests band together. The members want to belong and they want to know the rest of the people by name. Friendships build because of this association. The group responds to the needs of one another and/or the wider community. There is a sense of inter-action between the members, a sense of identification with the group. Not everyone is at every meeting, but they generally are in attendance. The focal point of this sort of grouping is not a mailing list, but a commitment to this group of people. The group does not exist merely for socializing but for the growth and development of the members.

Such a community provides an atmosphere that assists personal growth. It is based primarily on personal relationships rather than programs or activities. It has many elements of a real community after the pattern of the gospel. Many groups might fit under this umbrella. The Christian Family movement, the Cursillo Movement, the Liturgical Movement or the Charismatic Movement are such communities. The people are drawn together by a clear interest in family life, liturgy, prayer or some sort of work. It was clear when someone belonged or did not. There was a sense of belonging but not necessarily a commitment to the group. This kind of community finds a constant turnover as people move in and out of it. There is no special organizational structure and few 'ties that bind.'

The difference between such a community and a basic Christian Community is partially in the fact of organization. The Basic Christian Community (BCC) creates an atmosphere and environment for growth and has enough organization to be able to function. It has gatherings of the community for development and formation. It also faces the danger of institutionalism and over-organizing. Yet, a community with solid organization, aware of the dangers of too much organization, can do great good in developing into a real Christian community. Any community without organization has a strength that comes from the fact that it is a voluntary grouping. But it is also weak, because it is at the mercy of the ups and downs of enthusiasm and changes in the environmental influences. It has no organization to hold it together if it begins to splinter, often no 'teeth' to call people to maintain a commitment.

The basic Christian community is an organism, aware and alert to the needs of its members. It is organized and can function as a unity and act. There is a commitment that is called for and responsible people to support and require the fulfillment of that commitment. It is not errorless, but neither is it at the whim of everything that comes along. It requires discipline of its members and must be constant in calling all members to continued growth and development. It has the backbone of organization to maintain its spirit and life. Those who belong to such a community are aware that it is not a 'sometime' thing.

But community, even gospel-community, does not simply happen through cheery good will and bland statements about loving one another. There must be a consuming vision, a dream, that is pursued by all who belong. The community has need of prophets who call it to return to the gospel life when it strays. It needs men and women of vision and faith who step out in new ventures that will witness the gospel life for right now! Nowhere will you find a perfect gospel community. Always you will find a community struggling to become such a community. Our call to follow Francis requires us to seek the struggle and share the burden and joy of building the community. It will do little good to have the special vision of Francis if we do not step out and do something about the vision. People who genuinely perceive the signs of the times and risk responding to it will help build the community. People whose physical activity is over will embrace suffering for the sake of the community. People who are at odds with one another in the fraternity will be called to reconciliation no matter how hard or how long the struggle. There is simply no ending to the process of building fraternity-community. In our humanness we will be detoured by many wasteful self-seekings. But we won't stop building because our callouses are hurting. The call Christ gave to Francis to "Repair my Church" applies as directly to us as it did to Francis. The constancy of personal renewal is tied directly to our commitment to building up the fraternity-community. Paul speaks wisely in his letter to the Galatians:

> My Brothers, remember that you have been called to live in freedom—but not a freedom that gives free rein to the flesh. Out of love, place yourselves at one another's service. The whole law has found its fulfillment in this one saying: "You shall love your neighbor as yourself." If you go on biting and tearing one another to pieces, take care! You will end up in mutual destruction.
>
> Galatians 5: 13 - 15

To work constantly to create the atmosphere and environment for growth in holiness requires faith in Jesus. Francis allowed a wide margin for the 'sinner' in man, yet he was disciplined and demanded self-control in his followers. He was willing to forgive seven times seventy times, but he could also understand that some men were called to follow a different way to holiness. God does the calling, but He asks us to examine and explore the calling so that we know that it is *our* calling. Seed needs time to germinate. But all seeds do not grow equally well in the same soil. It is the responsibility of the Franciscan community to recognize the authenticity of the individual's call.

Fraternity gathers together a variety of people under the banner of Francis. In the fraternity each person is called, not to do his own thing, but to do the one seraphic thing in his own unique way. This fraternity-community needs to be sensitive to the uniqueness of each individual. Our richness comes from helping each person develop into the person he can be. It is not our call to mold everyone into the same monolithic pattern.

> It was part of Francis' genius that he could inspire men of differing temperaments, from the most diverse backgrounds, and of the most variant views to achieve the closest fraternal unity while each remained gloriously himself. Even more, while each one grew to be more gloriously himself and less ingloriously a caricature of God's creative work in him.

> St Francis was as realistically aware of Masseo's vanity as of Rufino's introvertedness; of Giles' sharp tongue as of Leo's curiosity. He did not wait until Masseo grew humble, Rufino outgoing, Giles sweet and Leo detached to form his fraternity. He took them as they were and helped them to become far better than they were. In this he showed how truly he was Francis of the gospel life, student of a realistic master.

> True realism is gentle, even in the beauty of its anger. It has taken men's measure and agreed to work with that size. It is when we are unrealistic enough to establish a measure to which men and situations must be fitted that we tend to become most aggressive about 'facing the reality of life.'
>
> Sister Mary Francis, *Cord*, April, 1970 117

Our community must possess at one and the same time a

deep sensitivity to the needs of men and a strong faith about the demands of God. It cannot water down the gospel to suit men, but help men to rise to the challenge of the gospel. It must require the members to be totally honest with themselves even when it hurts and must walk with the weak so that they experience God's loving care. There will always be tension in a Franciscan community, but it will be a creative tension. It will push and call the members to reach out for things they had never imagined they would do and stand ready to walk with them to achieve the dream. The Franciscan community will experience the tension that comes when we recognize human weakness but do not allow it to be an excuse to avoid growth. There will be acceptance and confrontation. Above all, there will be the prayerful tension that leads us beyond human expectations to the enormous and secure risk of trusting God completely. The only how-to-do-it book for such a community is the gospel and it is our way of life.

On the personal level we shall experience the work it takes to close the gap between what we read in the gospel and what we do in our life. It will require more than intellectual discussion and move us to total participation in living the gospel. We would like to have the community for support but we might want to be independent when we feel we don't need it. We will experience the tension of coming to grips with this feeling in the light of our call to follow Francis. We want to grow in personal intimacy with Jesus but we may be surprised at some of the unexpected ways that we will be asked to walk to achieve intimacy. We want so much for ourselves, and we are called to die to self in order to live. The Franciscan community is a place of paradox. It is a community where loving acceptance and firm discipline exist side by side. It is a community where pettiness can exist side-by-side with total self-giving. It is a community that can get bogged down in people-projects and yet be called repeatedly to deeper prayer. It is a place of struggle and peace, where men and women, young and old, sometimes plod and sometimes dash in their pursuit of the dream of Francis. We believe that when our Father calls us to such a dream, he furnishes the wherewithal to accomplish it. If we must be buried with Christ in order to rise with him, so be it. Faith tells us that this is our way to God. Hope nourishes us to seek to achieve it. Love drives us to make the dream come true in us, the little ones.

Community living puts us in direct touch with many different people. Some will be agreeable, some less so. We shall be expected to reach out to all in the best way we are able. Here too we will find that if we consider ourselves worthless, we may have trouble relating to others. If I have what I consider 'nothing' or very little, I may not want to risk what little I have. So I can put on a façade of neighborly love without getting personally involved. We can waste much time avoiding real commitment.

Here again the Franciscan community needs to create an atmosphere of acceptance that helps the individual overcome this fear. Honest and warm love, support and acceptance need to be evident qualities in a Franciscan fraternity. They will be joined to the qualities of forgiveness, patience, compassion, understanding, peace-making and a large capacity for frustration. Our Franciscan community will always be *trying* to create a warm atmosphere of acceptance. It will be constantly succeeding and failing in this effort, winning and losing in this struggle. It is not a perfect community. But it must always be stretching itself to be more perfect than it is as it reaches for the dream of Francis.

> To take life as it is, and people as they are . . . is the only way to achieve anything positive, beautiful and good in human situations, and actually to change life or men. But it takes an utter realist to do it. It is so much easier to whine, revolt, sit down (or in), commit murder or suicide.
>
> Sister Mary Francis *Cord* April, 1970 119

Francis has shown us a way of life that leads to Jesus. The values of that life are unlimited, the demands constant. But they lead, finally, to Jesus and his Father and the Spirit—the community of joy and hope and love and life.

The ways and means of fraternity life can change and fluctuate. Fraternity life itself must always grow. We take our calling seriously. So we shall be realistic about our need for community and for each other as part of that community. This community must be known for the warmth of its love and its responsiveness to the needs of men. But it will never forget that the first commandment calls us to love God with everything we are. We need Jesus. We are nothing without him. Our own weakness makes it clear that he alone is savior. No community will ever become a Christian community without Christ. No Franciscan community-fraternity shall ever grow without Christ. No Franciscan can contribute to that growth without strong personal attachment to Jesus Christ. Oneness is the fruit of the Spirit of Jesus. We cannot do it alone.

A group of people that is really a community, can do great things whether it is large or small. A small group has the advantage of deeply personal relationships. It is simpler for the relationships to go to a deeper level than may be possible with large groups of people in community. But a large group that is really a community can accomplish things far beyond the means of a small community. The variety in a large group can add vitality to the community. It can provide a breadth of experience that a small group cannot provide. A small group, on the other hand, can find a depth in relationships that a large group cannot. Both can be solid communities and Franciscans will work to accomplish community in either case.

There is often a confusion about the meaning of words regarding community. It is quite legitimate to speak of community life as family life. There are, however, a number of specific differences between ordinary family life and community life in a fraternity. In the ordinary fraternity, the members do not live together in the same place. Communication cannot be taken for granted, therefore, nor left until tomorrow because fraternity members don't always see each other that often. A family has a great deal of togetherness (physical) that a fraternity must achieve by close personal relationships that can tolerate physical absence. The demands are different and the term 'family' can confuse the issue. Being brothers in the spirit is not the same as being blood brothers. It is unwise to imagine that the same relationship would exist between adults as between parents and children in a family. The Councilors in a fraternity are not parents nor are the members children. Family concepts can do damage to this understanding. The expressions of intimacy within family life can be quite different than the natural response of Franciscans to one another. Families differ greatly in the way in which affection, love and caring is shown. Lumping a fraternity into the concept of 'family' will mean confusion about such ways and means. The term 'community' is a wise one as is the term 'brotherhood.' Both express the gospel ideal of Francis. If the term family is used, it should be clearly spelled out what is meant. Fraternity life is not the same as family life even though there are mutual qualities required by both.

We follow Jesus not only to Mount Tabor and glorification but also to Mount Calvary and crucifixion. In learning how to die, we learn how to live. Jesus calls us to life, and death to self is the doorway to such life.

It is invariably only the dying man who appreciates to the full the beauty and joy of life. This seems to be the healthy and invigorating idea which is struggling to extricate itself from the 'new look' in mortification.

In the same way that really great Christian humorists always take God very seriously, St Francis was joyous in poverty, gay in self-discipline, bent on losing his life so that he might save it. He always took God at his word and so he thought that falling into the furrow of earth's sorrows in order to bring forth much fruit not at all an unattractive modus vivendi.

Marginals, Sister Mary Francis 66

So we are called to junk our opinionated ideas and the non-essentials that keep us from Jesus. Francis speaks loudly to us as we build up community life. Don't be fooled by appearances! Get to the heart of things. At no time can we let up and say we have a right to rest. Work while there is light!

To my dying day, however, I will not cease at least by example and good endeavor to teach the brothers how to tread the course the Lord has shown me, the course I have till now, by word and example, taught and shown them, so that they are inexcusable before the Lord and I am not bound further to render an account for them before God.

Words of St Francis, #260

9. The Bigger the Better

PEOPLE ARE A PART OF LIFE. Each of us is a 'people' and yet we can find other 'people' hard to understand. Within our Fraternity life we will have to work at understanding each other. We need to grow in our responsiveness to the needs of others. Personality will play a part in how we do this. But there are some ways and means that can help us in building relationships.

One element that is important is that we put into practice what we profess to follow. A deepening intimacy with Jesus ought to show in our dealings with others. It ought to show in the way we respond to day-to-day situations at work, at home, in school or wherever we may be. Jesus will call us to more and more fulfillment of his gospel. Within the fraternity we will likewise need to show that Jesus is helping us change. To help us in some of these group relationships, we want to examine a few things that might be of help.

There are a number of elements involved in group growth: 1) A recognition of the need for *personal* growth; 2) An understanding of the process by which the group builds itself or group building; 3) The need for the group to take realistic action.

No group is going to grow if the individuals remain stagnant. Any group depends on its members for development. But this is especially true in our Franciscan Fraternity life. The manner in which each of us uses our gifts of personality, ability and desire will help to shape the tone of the fraternity. The kind of hang-ups, fears and weaknesses that are yours will make a difference in the growth and development of fraternity life. If you come to fraternity life only to receive, you will simply deplete the group treasury. If you never share, you become a drain on fraternity life. If you come in order to give the gift of yourself, to share the things that are yours, then you are a builder of fraternity life. Your decision will make the difference. There is an evident correlation between the generosity of the members and the growth of true fraternity life. Individual growth is important to fraternity growth. The group-builders process draws on the trust that the people within the fraternity have for each other. When we speak of a group developing and moving along in growth, there is a need for all the members to want to move in a particular direction. So long as people drag their feet, the group growth is slowed down. Group building will require honest and responsible sharing. Honest, because the truth alone can set us free; responsible, because the sharing must be in accord with the ability of the group to be a sharing community at any moment. To rush headlong into sharing on a deep feeling level may be very truthful, but irresponsible if the group is not ready for that. Trust requires confidentiality about fraternity affairs that we share on a personal level. The deeper we move into the feeling level of sharing, the greater the need for each of us to be worthy of the confidence another shows by revealing his inner self. Group building will require a great deal of patience. Not everyone is ready to move at the same time. Here is where honest and responsible communication is so vital. People need to know what is being asked of them. They need to be free to question the direction the group is taking. They need to be at ease with the decision so they can support it. Dictates from on high will not move the group. It assures an external conformity, but if the heart is not in it, the dictate might as well never have been made, for the group is not really moving with it.

Anyone who works with groups knows the importance of

communication and real dialogue. Any people who guide the group must be deeply sensitive to the feelings of the people in the fraternity. In Franciscan fraternity life, no one should ever ride roughshod over the feelings of others. A human person is a fragile thing. Using gimmicks of any kind to manipulate people into movement is not our way. Francis calls us to a deep respect for every person. Franciscans have the right to expect such individual, caring treatment from their leadership. Here again, we must walk between the extremes of dictatorial demands and wishy-washy nonsense. Leaders must lead! But the timetable of leadership is often not something that can be determined beforehand. Franciscan leadership takes the pulse of the people and pushes in directions sought by the members and/or holds out horizons the members may not have considered. But the moment that leaders become spiritual bulldozers; or when they simply want their own thing without concern for the members, then the leader needs to re-evaluate his or her personal growth. Gentleness, warmth, firmness must be the arsenal of a Franciscan leader. To be a servant of all is to be ready to listen to all and be responsive to need.

The fraternity, like any group, will need to take responsible action both as a group and individually. This is not the same as substituting work for prayerfulness. Prayer is one of our most vital activities. But we speak here of the need to act as well as speak and discuss. A creative Franciscan group will find plenty to do. No matter where you are, people have needs that we can meet. Were a fraternity to do nothing but be a devotional society, it would already have lost its right to be called Franciscan. Sometimes we become spiritual gluttons, feasting on the meat of our Franciscan riches without ever sharing it with others. That cannot be tolerated. The solid life and love of any fraternity worth its salt will find expression in the works of love. There are many degrees of involvement. A good fraternity will have possible action for all the members; action geared to the abilities of the membership. Human need and the cry of the poor must take special place in our work. In today's world of injustice, oppression, loneliness, callousness, impersonalism and a sort of dis-engagement from personal involvement, Franciscans must be willing to walk with the poor. Franciscans must be companions to the lonely. Franciscans must be involved with the dis-enfranchised. Franciscans must be in the jails and prisons where men and women often lose hope and prey on one another. Franciscans must be where houses are cold and children ill-clothed and poorly fed. Franciscans must be on committees to alleviate poverty and racism and inhumanity of man to man. Franciscans will not worry about headlines, only about what is happening in the heart of those whom they try to serve. Sponsoring events of prayer are good. Saying rosaries and listening to talks at workshops are fine. But sooner or later, the real Franciscan shall need to stop listening and begin to share God's gifts with those who are poor. It is the way to wholeness. We do not question and discuss forever whether we shall work *or* pray. Rather, we know that we must work *and* pray, and we will.

Trying to keep the three ingredients of group process in proportion is not easy. At different times there may be a need to stress one in preference to the other. Some groups seem to spend all their time in study and prayer. They can get spiritual indigestion because they fail to share the riches that study and prayer can bring. Other groups talk about social problems but never do anything about it. They are bankrupt. Other groups are so hyper-active that they miss each other in the whirlwind of activity and have no time for solid personal growth. Their activity soon deteriorates into plain, dull 'work' and loses its ability to enrich life. It is a wise fraternity that takes time periodically to examine where it stands in this regard. The Franciscan must be a realist. We cannot do everything. In fact, without Christ we can do nothing. So we are clearly called to a realistic awareness of the need for prayer. But when Jesus comes close to us in prayer, he makes us aware of the needs of his little people and sends us to serve them. The Franciscan is one who takes time to stand still before God and is sent to walk with his brother. That is the balance we seek, for it is the reality of the gospel life. The same Jesus who walked the roads of Palestine healing and teaching and taking time for people, also woke up early in the morning and went to a lonely place and prayed there to his Father. Care came from the Father. Strength to continue caring will have to continue to come from the Father.

RANDOM IDEAS ON THE GROUP AND I

There are different levels of relationship with others. In ordinary life we move back and forth between these levels, depending on the situation and the people involved. One degree of relationship is the 'lip-service' conversation. Here we talk about all sorts of things, none of which are very personal. No deep feelings are revealed. At best we simply comment on the passing scene without really saying too much about where we stand. The weather; the fall colors of the leaves; football; modern problems, and on and on we drone. It is the normal sort of thing for people who do not know one another very well or who have not yet built trust. On another level of sharing is the mind-to-mind sort of sharing. It is more serious than the first and begins to touch the edges of our self. But we keep it pretty much in the realm of ideas and opinions, often abstractions, about many things. Engrossing conversations on the spiritual life; talks about the theory of prayer; general investigation about the gospels. In short, it is a serious conversation, but most often still impersonal and rather academic. We deal with things mainly on an intellectual level and enjoy the give and take of good argument about various opinions on various topics. Most often we shall not talk about how we *feel* about the opinions we express. Another level of communication is the heart-to-heart sharing. It is the honest, open sharing of one's real self with another. We speak honestly about our feelings. We share the inner fears we may have, or express the joys that touch our hearts. We show this inner expression through tears or anger or whatever because we want the other to know our inner self. It is real communing with another. It is at this level that community reaches its zenith, for here we face the truth about ourselves, the gospel and Jesus, and each other. Here we show trust and acceptance, compassion and understanding, gentleness and awareness. It is here that silence becomes the vehicle of communication.

The different levels of relationship and communication will be part of ordinary life. As fraternity life deepens people will begin to say to each other: "This is the way I feel;" "In all honesty this is where I am." "This is me, I want to be part of you and for you to be part of me." When this level of sharing is part of fraternity life real growth will take place. It is a level of trust that happens very slowly and cannot be rushed. Every Franciscan Fraternity must work to create the sort of environment and atmosphere that will help build trusting relationships. It is important to know that this process will always be going on and each of us will contribute to it. If we hold back, the fraternity will be slowed down in its growth.

If we wish to reach this communing level of sharing we need to know some of the requirements. When anyone finally feels free enough to share his inner self, he is very fragile at that moment. Whoever is present is in the presence of the blossoming of something precious, the heart of another person. We need to respect such a trust. When someone wishes to share in this way, never interrupt them! Allow them the freedom to speak their heart. Most often they are not looking for advice or cliches. They simply want to be listened to and accepted. So never start giving advice or interrupting when this revealing of self is happening. Listen with all your heart and the mouth will keep quiet. Leave room for more sharing so that everything that needs to be shared is shared. Sometimes in these situations we are tempted to become detectives of the heart. This is definitely not the time to probe and prod. Probing forces the person to reveal things they may wish not to reveal. Do not push into the tender secrets of another's heart. Don't let anyone else do it either. Probing may be the drug that will forever close off any future sharing.

All of us like to give advice whether we ought to or not. Whenever there is a deep sense of sharing, advice is not needed nor is it welcome. If you wish, you might share a personal experience that matches what is shared. But simply share it and allow the person the freedom to take your experience or leave it alone. Far too often we give advice without really hearing what is being said. Sharing one's deepest feelings with another is a time when we look simply for acceptance and not advice. Even when we know there is no solution, we need to know that someone else has heard us and understood. How easy it can be to judge the action or feeling of another. Again, judgement is not the quality that is needed here. Simple acceptance is what we are after in these areas of deep-level sharing of self. As Franciscans, we ought to treat the revelations of another as a precious jewel of trust and protect and cherish it with all our heart. It is a pearl of great price.

In developing our relationships with people, especially within a community, we will need the quality of flexibility. A maturing person will show such a quality because he is more realistic about life and people. The person who is rigid in his thinking will have to manipulate and control people. Otherwise he may have to change a rigid opinion and that might destroy him! The rigid person will find people moving away from him. More and more he will be left alone. There is no life in him. Opinions and ideas are firmly set and hard as concrete. Warmth and openness are unknown quantities with him.

Flexibility is a sensitive response to others; a recognition of goodness in others no matter how deeply it is hidden. The flexible person has hope that change is possible, both in himself and in others. Flexibility gives the good seed room to grow. It calls for a trust of others. When we seek the good in another we are likely to trust in that goodness. We do not need to label people or box them into stereotypes in order to feel secure. We are free enough to risk treating others with trust and freedom and accepting the consequences of such risks.

The rigid person, on the other hand, is fearful of any kind of change. He cannot control the situation if he allows for change. A rigid person can control the future by clinging to the past. Or he can control by ignoring the past and imposing new structures on others with no concern for anyone but himself. The world is a frightening place for a rigid person. As things keep changing around him, he becomes more fearful and insecure. His response to the threat of change is to become more rigid. We commonly call this freezing, polarization. When we mistrust people we become indecisive and insecure on the inside and hide this by an apparent absoluteness on the outside. A rigid person cannot share his inner self because he cannot even share that reality with himself. In one way or another, the rigid person lives in a world of fear; a world that tends to grow smaller and more threatening all the time. A rigid Franciscan would be an apparent contradiction. Following the gospel requires openness to the Spirit. Such openness will lead to unexpected places known only to the Spirit. A rigid person would find it most difficult to accept the risk of the unknown path pointed out by the Spirit. The flexible person can move out readily, able to accept risk and change as a natural consequence of being a gospel person.

Franciscans must be a people who are aware of life and its wonders. We are aware when there is hesitancy in speaking about certain topics. We gently leave those topics alone for

the moment. We sense the spirit of joy and sparkle when a
good experience is shared and we delight with the one who
is sharing. We sense the silent withdrawal when a painful
subject arises and simply share a silent moment of support
with one another. We are aware of the embarrassment of
another and help them over the hurdle. We sense the fears
that sometimes show in loud aggressiveness or an apparent
calm and we respond to the fear and not the noise. When
another has been hurt and reconciliation is needed, we must
sense this need and move toward reconciliation no matter
how great the price or how long the journey. A Franciscan
notices the shy advances and withdrawals of someone who is
new to fraternity life and moves to show them acceptance.
When anger and accusation rear their ugly heads in fraternity
life, the aware Franciscan moves to find a way to defuse and
re-direct the power at work.

St Francis could never see a mob of people. He always
sorted them out and saw the individual person. He could not
accept the ideas of mass-conversions in approaching people.
Rather, he wanted each person he touched to know that he
was known by name. Francis did not manipulate people
through psychological or emotional means. Instead, he was
willing to walk alongside any man who sought to find God.
It is part of our rich Franciscan heritage that we are a people
concerned for each individual. To that individual we bring
our own love and warmth, big or little as it may be. But
never do we lump people together and treat them as a 'lump'
of people. As followers of Francis we shall seek to discover
the delicate balance between awareness and probing; honesty
and being overbearing; sensitive response and impersonal
probing. Each of us has blundered with words we wish we
could draw back. There is always risk in dealing with our own
feelings and those of others. But the risk will not deter
us from growing in our awareness and sensitivity to
others. We are little brothers and servants to one
another.

If we are to be
We must be where we are, who we are, what we are.
We cannot be otherwise and be real.

Yet, without dreams, we are boxed in by our own
limitations.
And the Lord knows our need to dream.
He pushed us to dream with him,
and walk with him, and be with him,
and be what he is.

To do that he gave us faith,
his gift of relationship with us,
frosted over with hope and love.

Always wanting, like us, to be whole and to be one.
And being for us in so many ways, but especially where
love is tested, on a cross
and in the stark nakedness of love laid open for us.

We must be one like Him and his Father.
We must forgive and reconcile,
be compassionate and trusting,
be open and honest and responsible,
so that we might be one
as Jesus prayed.

Our Franciscan fraternity life will call for much virtue. We
are a sinful people reaching out to be holy. It is possible, but
the seeking is never finished. Each of us will find some things
within us that hurts or hinders another. We shall struggle to
change and sometimes even refuse to struggle. The Fraternity
will call us to face reality, and we may rebel. Always, then,
among these people who seek perfection through the Franciscan way of life, we will be in tension. Tension created by
the struggle of seeing what we really are and knowing what

we ought to be; and the difficulty of embracing the wholeness the gospel requires. But we shall not be alone. We
shall be with friends who will allow the tension to lead us
upward and not backward. It shall be good for we shall
walk together, roped to Jesus.

10. Sounds of Silence

THE SPIRIT OF GOD GIVES LIFE. He reaches into the depths of a man to help him discover reality. With a gentle breath of power, the Spirit captures us like the wind captures a leaf and moves us to things beyond our wildest dreams. With unexpected freshness he reveals a dimension of life that was unknown. With the searing flame of his love and the power of his gifts he hones and sharpens us for living. We are breathless in his hands and he becomes our life. As the eagle takes her young on her wings high into the sky and drops them so they might learn how to fly, so does the Spirit lift us up. As the eagle swoops again and again to catch her young lest they are hurt, so does the Spirit of God gently teach us how to fly with the Father.

Prayer takes our life and gives it to the Father. Prayer is not simply a good feeling that comes to us, though the Spirit may grant us that. Prayer is not the dark nights of emptiness and abandonment, though such nights might be part of our way to the Father. Prayer is not judged simply by the presence or absence of feelings. Rather, it is judged by life. Real prayer gives a perspective to life, making us more aware of the call of the Father who is my Father.

In the musical: "Man of La Mancha" there is a dialogue between Alonso Chiana and the prostitute-turned-lady Aldonza that expresses the power of a loving relationship. Aldonza, bar maid and free-wheeling prostitute was touched by the strange respect that Don Quixote (Chiana's dream identity) had given her. He saw the prostitute Aldonza as a

Lady and addressed her as such. He called her 'My Lady, Dulcinea.' She is puzzled and angry at first. She cannot understand this madman. Yet, she is strangely attracted to this man who treats her so well despite the externals. A bond, as yet nameless, grows between them. Toward the end of the musical, the dream world of Don Quixote had been shattered and poor old, addle-headed Alonso Chiana is dying in his family's home. Aldonza, the prostitute breaks into the room of the dying man.

Alonso does not recognize her. He is weak and sick and confused by shadows. "I do not know you!" Aldonza speaks out again the agonizing question: "Don't you know me?" "Is it so important?" he replies. "Everything," answers Aldonza: "My whole life! You spoke to me and everything seemed different!" "I spoke to you?" whispers Alonso. "Yes, and you called me by another name, Dulcinea." All the longing inside the human heart of Aldonza springs out to share herself with Alonso. His acceptance of her; his calling her a 'Lady' awakened something in her that she thought could never be. She began to believe that she is Dulcinea. Everything is seen fresh and different because she has been touched by a creative love of a dreamy old man called Don Quixote.

Prayer does such things to us. It binds us to a Father who believes in us and sends his Spirit in response to his Son's plea. Our growth in prayer is measured by our deepening awareness of the Father. "He speaks to us and everything seems different!" Jesus calls us to unity with the Father and the Spirit. You and I will need to open our hearts to this God. It is the Aldonza in each of us being called a Dulcinea by a loving God.

We pray where we are. That is the starting point, for where life is, there is the Spirit and there shall he touch us. Since this is so, our responsibility calls us to look at ourselves where we are.

There are many enemies of prayer. One of the most

penetrating modern enemies is noise, or perhaps, the lack of silence. Amplifiers and transistors follow us everywhere. Noise has become a way of life for many and silence has been assassinated. Yet there is still in the human heart that longing for a space for silence. People still need to stop and reflect; to let the sounds of creation seep into their heart and imagination and memory. But many are afraid to be quiet. Many seem to run away from time to be alone with themselves. Insecure, anxious; they dare not risk discovering some of the emptiness within. Such fear is an enemy to prayer. Prayer will need times of silence. We will need to 'stand still' before God and listen to his voice in the whisper of the wind. Jesus sought such times for silence so that he might commune with the Father. It kept Him tuned to the will of the Father and gave him the courage to fulfill that will in his life.

Though noise is a problem in prayer, the attitude about success is also a problem. We are almost saturated with the philosophy of 'instant success.' Things are moving so fast that if we are not immediately able to see the results of what we do, we feel that we are wasting our time. Nothing can wait. We must do it now! Prayer does not indulge this fancy of ours. The calm of prayer often requires a long period of waiting on God. Prayer calls us to an atmosphere of acceptance of God's timetable. So often that is far different than the 'instant success' philosophy dictates. The craze of having everything right away can be a large barrier to the gentle paced working of the Spirit in prayer. Coupled with this barrier is the gnawing fear that sometimes enters us when we pray. Little by little the Spirit draws us to a wider vision and a more complete yielding to the Father. But we begin to sense that it will finally mean yielding everything into his hands. The tug of the Spirit is felt, but the consequence of response seems too much to accept. Without always knowing why, we know that he will turn our life inside out if we allow it. Deep within our heart we know that he will transform every fiber of our life. We sense that he will lead us in directions we never expected to go. Sometimes the vision frightens us. The things we have look so good. The people around us seem so necessary to continued living. Our present job seems like the only one that can bring joy. Prayer may bring us to leave that country of things and people and tasks to go to a place he shall show us. Prayer requires of us the faith of an Abraham and we feel very weak-kneed about the whole thing.

But in the quiet recesses of real prayer we will begin to see things differently and yield to the call of the Spirit. It shall be a battle between all the human excuses and rationalizations and the absolute imperiousness of the call of the Spirit. The combat between faith and hope and love on the one side and selfishness, pride and plain fright on the other shall be no simple battle. What will happen if I do say "Yes"? Where will it lead? No blueprint is likely to be forthcoming from our Father. No magical formulas nor instant success. What will happen is that the Father will continue to call us to respond to his all-embracing; "I love you." In the light of that creative love we are strangely attracted and afraid at the same time. We had not dreamed that prayer would bring us to such a point.

Beyond doubt prayer will deepen faith and rely on faith for its growth. We accept the love of the Father and the power of the Spirit. In the naked awareness of the Father's will, we cry with Jesus: "If it is possible, take this cup from me!" We will say it again and again and plead with Jesus to help us finish that prayer: "Not my will, but yours be done." We need to come to Jesus to pray this way. We need to lay ourselves open to the molding power of the Spirit. We listen in wonder to the word of the Lord to Jeremiah in the potters house: "Can I not do to you, house of Israel, as this potter has done?" says the Lord. "Indeed like clay in the hand of the potter, so are you in my hand . . ." (Jeremiah 18: 6) If this is where prayer leads, we can understand why it is so demanding. We are not accustomed to being dependent. We are taught independence. Prayer will bring us to the point of total dependence on God. It will bring us to leave behind anything that possesses us or about which we are possessive. We will be clay in the hands of God, ready to be molded into the vessel of service he chooses for us. As we honestly seek such a 'handing over' to the Lord, we shall also discover the peace he promises to those who really love him. Having found what we lost, we shall simply celebrate and praise our God for his wonders.

The manner in which the Jewish people prayed at the time of Jesus gives us some ideas about prayer. Jesus himself learned to pray in this way. The devout Hebrew took time to pray at least three times each day. On rising in the morning, his prayer was a hymn of praise for the day that stretched out before him. In the afternoon, in the midst of his day, he prayed that he might remember the source of his life and work, Yahweh. He prayed before he retired in the evening, thanking God for the gifts of the day. Jesus prayed in this manner each day. So did his apostles. Taking time for Yahweh gave purpose and meaning to the day.

The form of these prayers is simple. It is called the "Blessings," or "Berakah." It began by a simple invocation, calling on Yahweh as the creator of all things. Then God was blessed and praised for his goodness both to individuals and to the people (nation) as a whole. Looking back on his personal and national history, man would recall the good things God had done in the past. Recalling this history helped man to see how God acts and what kind of God he is. This touch with the good things of the past revealed God's plan more clearly. After calling these good things to mind, the prayer moved from praise and thanks to petition. Since Yahweh has been so good in the past, we have reason to hope that he will hear my present petition. The petition for help asks God to continue to show his power and majesty by answering the petition. Finally, the Berakah concluded with another praise of Yahweh.

This prayer is simple and personal, but never isolated from the sense of unity with all of God's people. Faith in Yahweh is based on all he has done for his people as well as what he has done for the individual. Even more dominant is the theme of praise and thanksgiving. A thing, a person is blessed by thanking God for it. This open praise of God helps us to a deeper willingness to accept God's plan for our lives. It deepens our faith in Yahweh and strengthens our dependence on the Father. It helps us to be sensitive to the way in which God works in life. To pray the Berakah consistently keeps us in touch with the Father's influence and calls us to respond to the will of the Father. Jesus himself used this form of prayer again and again in his life. It was a source of power and strength for him. How often he spoke of the need to be consistent and constant in our prayer.

Jesus said to them: "If one of you knows someone who comes to him in the middle of the night and says to him: 'Friend, lend me three loaves, for a friend of mine has come in from a journey and I have nothing to offer him.' And he from inside should reply: 'Leave me alone. The door is shut now and my children and I are in bed. I cannot get up to look after your needs.' I tell you, even though he does not get up and take care of the man because of friendship, he will do so because of his persistence, and give him as much as he needs.

So, I say to you, 'Ask, and you shall receive; seek and you shall find; knock and it will be opened to you. For whoever asks, receives; whoever seeks, finds; whoever knocks, is admitted. What father among you will give his son a snake if he asks for a fish, or hand him a scorpion if he asks for an egg? If you, with all your sins, know how to give your children good things, how much more will the heavenly Father give the Holy Spirit to those who ask him.

Luke 11: 5 - 13

Faith leads us to continue in prayer. Prayer helps our faith and trust to grow. Jesus says clearly that the Father shall give the Holy Spirit to those who ask him. One obvious consequence of prayer is that we receive and/or become more sensitive to the Spirit. With the coming of the Spirit into our heart, there will be a more generous acceptance of the will of the Father. This in turn will lead to the conversion within us that shall open another attic corner of our life to the action of the Spirit.

There is something special about the prayer that Jesus taught his apostles. Both Jesus and the apostles knew the Berakah prayer. When they asked Jesus to teach them to pray, they were asking for something that would have a 'special touch' to it that would identify them as followers of Jesus. Jesus taught them this way:

When you pray, say: "Father, hallowed be your name, your kingdom come. Give us each day our daily bread. Forgive us our sins for we too forgive all who do us wrong; and subject us not to the trial.

Luke 11: 2 - 4

This is how you are to pray: Our Father in heaven, hallowed be your name, your kingdom come, your will be done on earth as it is in heaven. Give us today our daily bread, and forgive us the wrong we have done as we forgive those who wrong us. Subject us not to the trial, but deliver us from the evil one.

Matthew 6: 9 - 13

The uniqueness of Jesus' prayer is the intimate way that it addresses God. He says directly and simply: "Our Father." It moves beyond being simply the Father of all mankind and makes us aware that he is my Father too. You are my God.

St Francis captured the sense of this prayer. He too was caught by the intimacy of the relationship with the Father. Francis spoke with an almost lyric quality in his personal reflections on the Our Father. His reflections on the phrase: "Your will be done on earth as it is in heaven" speak of the total kind of response he sought:

> . . . so that we may love you with all our heart by always keeping you in mind; with all our soul, by always longing for you; with all our mind, by directing all our intentions to you and seeking your glory in everything; and with all our strength by exerting all the forces and faculties of soul and body in your loving service and in nothing else. So may we love our neighbors as ourselves, by getting them all, so far as we can, to love you, by being glad at the good fortune of others as at our own, while feeling for their misfortune, and giving no offense to anybody.
>
> *Words of St Francis*, #36

Francis knew the gospels well. He knew how frequently Jesus took time to commune with his Father. He heard Jesus' words to us: "No one can come to the Father except through me." So prayer brings us to Jesus who teaches us about the Father who in turn floods our lives by sending the Spirit. Jesus reveals the Father in many different parables and reflections. He shows his Father as a forgiving Father in the parable of the Prodigal son. He asks us to trust this Father completely when he speaks of how much more important we are than the lilies of the fields or the birds of the air. He speaks of the intimacy he has with the Father and how the Father and he are one. It is the Father who prepares many mansions for us. Jesus returns to the Father so that he might send the Spirit to us and prepare a place for us. Jesus asks us to be perfect like the Father is perfect. He prays to the Father in the moment of absolute agony and aloneness on the cross. It is the Father, always the Father, whose influence dominates the life and actions of the human Jesus. Jesus, the man-God, is the window through which we see the Father as he really is. In Jesus we discover the tender care of the Father for his people. In Jesus we see the pattern of the Father's love, a pattern that moves through suffering to resurrection and life. Real prayer brings us to follow this pattern in love, never getting bogged down in self-pity when the Father chooses an unexpected way to draw us to himself. How carefully Jesus reveals his Father as the foundation of his strength and power. The many times that Jesus goes to a 'lonely place' to pray are the times of renewal for him.

> I give you my assurance, whatever you ask the Father, he will give you in my name. Until now you have not asked for anything in my name. Ask and you shall receive, that your joy may be full. I have spoken these things to you in veiled language. A time will come when I shall no longer do so, but shall tell you about the Father in plain speech. On that day you will ask in my name and I do not say that I will petition the Father for you. The Father already loves you, because you have loved me and have believed that I came from God.
> John 16: 23 - 28

The power of prayer lies in its ability to free us from clinging to human limitations and moving to the Father's horizons. The power of prayer lies in its ability to free us from fear and any kind of self-help sort of half-truth to embrace the reality of total dependence on the Father. The power of prayer lies in its ability to teach us how to yield to the Father and thus to experience the calm and peace promised by Jesus when we believe in him. The power of prayer lies in its ability to help us face the full possibility of the faith-life instead of languishing in the twilight of mere human knowledge. The power of prayer lies in its ability to draw us to the Father and to open us to the Spirit. Prayer brings us to praise the Lord through Jesus Christ.

> Because you are God's chosen ones, holy and beloved, clothe yourselves with heartfelt mercy, with kindness, humility, meekness and patience. Bear with one another; forgive whatever grievances you have against one another. Forgive as the Lord has forgiven you. Over all these virtues put on love, which binds the rest together and makes them perfect. Christ's peace must reign in your hearts, since as members of the one body you have been called to that peace. Dedicate yourselves to thankfulness. Let the word of Christ, rich as it is, dwell in you. In wisdom made perfect, instruct and admonish one another. Sing gratefully to God from your hearts in psalms, hymns, and inspired songs. Whatever you do, whether in speech or in action, do it in the name of the Lord Jesus. Give thanks to God the Father through him.
>
> Colossians 3: 12 - 17

Prayer brings us to life and to all that faith-life requires of us in dealing with one another. Prayer brings us to the understanding of the saying of Jesus that the seed must die before it can bear fruit. Above all, prayer finally frees us from the prison of self-seeking to the seeking of the praise of God.

> In him we were chosen; for in the decree of God, who administers everything according to his will and counsel, we were predestined to praise his glory by being the first to hope in Christ. In him you too were chosen; when you heard the glad tidings of salvation, the word of truth, and believed in it, you were sealed with the

Holy Spirit who had been promised. He is the pledge of our inheritance, the first payment against the full redemption of a people God has made his own, to praise his glory.

Ephesians 1: 11 - 14

We glory, therefore, as sons and daughters of our heavenly Father. We are his, we belong to him, and we shall bear with us the influence of the Father. Wherever we go, whatever we do, we are a people of the Spirit, sent to proclaim the love of the Father as shown through Jesus Christ.

Most holy Lord, I should like to love you. Dearest God, I should like to love you. O Lord God, I have given up to you all my heart and my body, and I yearn passionately to do still more for love of you, if only I knew how!

Words of St Francis, #23

Once again we discover the importance of the Scriptures. If prayer brings us to seek the Father's will, the Scriptures are his living word to us through Jesus. We follow Jesus. We look in the word of the Lord for the pattern of our own life. We 'eat' the Scriptures and take them into our heart so that we can express their message in what we do and say and are. The gospel way of life is a natural consequence of prayer because it is the way of Jesus.

Our Franciscan way of life requires us to develop a prayerfulness in our lives. Each day we need to take time for God, and our Franciscan way of life requires this of us. It adds the discipline of requirement to the vision of our desire to know the Father. It is a support to our need for support. We easily drift away from developing prayerfulness in our lives. There are so many other things that seem more important on any given day. There are all those times when we don't 'feel' like praying. There is the ever-present devil of procrastination and/or self-seeking that gets in the way of taking time for prayer. When we run away from God we are simply tired and empty. Only in the Father's arms will we find peace and joy and freedom.

"Is it so important?" asks Alonso. "Everything! My whole life. You spoke to me and everything seemed different!" The transformation of Aldonza into a Dulcinea is a tribute to the power of faith and love. The Father can work such transformation in our lives too. It is because Francis sought such a transformation that he discovered Jesus and his gospel as the way to life. Franciscans of every age continue to make that discovery as they pray.

> We seek, Lord, to stay strangers, lest knowing Thee we would have nothing else.
> We skirt the fringes of your mansions, Lord,
> Afraid that living for you might bring a direction and growth that will bring the cross.
> We are frightened of you, Lord, you are so demanding.
> Yet, for all our running away, it is You we seek.
> For all our intellectualism, it is You we want.
> And for all our rationalizations, it is You we believe.
> Maybe, Lord, just maybe,
> we will begin to be free enough to say "Yes" to you.
> Free enough to fly, like the eagle, to see reality as you see it so that we can live life as you call us to do.
>
> Lord, teach us to pray.

11. I Love How You Love Me

FRANCIS OF ASSISI WAS AN OPTIMIST. His optimism was not blind to evil in the world, but he believed that the power of Jesus far surpassed the power of evil. So Francis was able to have a solid hope in the possibilities of any individual to come to God through the man-God.

Jesus often spoke about the power of love. He asks his followers to love God totally and to love one's neighbor and to love one's self. These three loves are the backbone of life with God. But the word 'love' conjures up many different images in our minds. In Scripture, love is the name for God. Love is unlimited, full of power to change, able to offer possibilities a whole lifetime could not exhaust. Francis pursued these discoveries with all his power. The capstone of this search came on Mount Alverna when Francis was sealed with the sign of the cross, the Stigmata. Francis shouted out his praise to the Father in the Canticle of Brother Sun. Yet even such wonders do not give us the full impact of the Father's love. Perhaps if we were to feel the full power of that loving Father, we would not be able to endure it and live. The Father's love is limited, in one way, by our capacity to receive. Yet even as we say this, we know that as long as we live we can expand our capacity to respond to the love of the Father. The whole of life offers new opportunities for insight and experience of the Father's love for us. Physical age can diminish the body's functions, but the spirit of man can grow stronger until the moment of death itself. The way of Jesus is a way of never ending search to be open to this

107

love and delighted by its surprises and expanded by its presence. Nature can reveal this love in the marvel of the tiniest form of life and the most delicate design. The Father's love is found in the power of tons of rock known as mountains or the surging, relentless force of the ocean. His love is found in the powerful wings of an eagle soaring high above the earth in splendid isolation or in the soft song of a canary, caged in the living room of a widow's home. Sunsets and animals, water and storm prompted a song of thanks from Francis of Assisi. For who can ever pay the price of one sunset?

But greater than the mountains or animals or sunsets is man. Each man, in his own way, reveals something of the unlimited wonder of the creator. In the humanness of man, we find the creative power of the creator. In man's goodness we see the reflection of God's goodness. Even the evil that man may do, draws a sharp contrast to the love the Father wants for us. Sin itself and the loneliness and emptiness it brings stands in sharp contrast to the fullness of love.

The world and creation and people are not simply 'means' to be used to find God. Rather, like man himself, they reveal something of the wholeness of God. To speak of "God's people" is to speak of the revelation of God through his action toward those he called his own. To seek the image of God around us is to discover the dignity of both creation and people. We do not discard creation or people in order to find God. Rather, both in creation and in people we find the need to keep on searching for the God who continues to reveal himself. The reflection keeps us aware of his faithful love and our own sinfulness. We know again that his love can re-create us.

There is mystery in this. There is so little proportion between our deserving and God's giving. There is so little proportion between the gifts we receive and the ones we return to the Father. Yet he has chosen us and given us dignity by the very relationship he established. The Father

considers us worthy of love. He has high hopes for us and
calls us to fulfill our potential. There is a marvel in the very
fact that the Father leaves us free to choose or refuse to be
his friend. He does not want a puppet; he will not be satisfied
with a chance acquaintanceship nor simply relating to a poor
clod of clay with a momentary chance for glory before passing
away. He calls us his friends and we can call him; "Father."
Such is the love of this God, calling us to be brother to Jesus,
temple and spouse of the Spirit and children of the Father
himself.

Some people never experience this love because they do
not wish to accept the cost. They are left free to refuse, but
they complain about their choice.

> They complain about their bad luck in not finding any
> friends or anyone who loves them, but it is not their
> bad luck, it is their fate. Having lost compassion and
> empathy, they do not touch anybody—nor can they be
> touched. Their triumph in life is not to need anybody.
> They take pride in their untouchability and pleasure in
> being able to hurt. Whether this is done in criminal or
> legitimate ways depends much more on social factors
> than on psychological ones. Most of them remain frozen
> and hence unhappy until their lives run out. Not so
> rarely, a miracle happens and a thaw begins.
>
> It may simply be that they meet a person whose
> concern and interest they believe, and new dimensions
> of feeling open. If they are lucky, they unfreeze com-
> pletely and the seeds of hope, which seem to have been
> destroyed altogether, come to life.
>
> *Revolution of hope*, Fromm 21

Our Father's love is the seed of hope that can unfreeze us.
It is the seed that blossomed in Francis' life. It showed in his
embrace of Lady poverty; in his delight with living; in his
contact with creation. Francis experienced the agony and

ecstacy of falling in love with God. Throughout his 44 years, Francis continued to discover the extent of the Father's love. Each new discovery brought another response from Francis and in turn led to another discovery. Little by little, brick by brick, stone by stone, Francis built the structure of his own love for the Father. It was not always a joyful discovery, operating at full steam. His spontaneity was not always clearsighted and brilliant. But the persistence of his pace led him to intimacy and intimacy led to a fuller response in love.

Francis deeply desired to remain in the times of solitude with the Lord. But he could not reconcile this desire with the example of Jesus in the gospel. Jesus went to his 'lonely place' but he returned to men enriched and shared those riches with the people. Francis did not choose either solitude or activity. He chose life as Jesus had lived it. In that life the times of solitude and the times of activity were partners. Life is incomplete when one is absent. Prayer taught him the secrets of the Father's love. He respected these personal contacts that were so very much his own. He knew that some moments are meant only for each other and no one else. He sensed the need for this kind of intimacy without losing sight of the need to share with others.

The call of Francis is an object lesson of the love of the Father. God took Francis, a quite ordinary man, and called him to do something special. The Father used all the qualities of generosity and impulsiveness that Francis possessed and directed them to the goal he sought for Francis. He re-created this young Italian through the power of his love. Francis, on his side, had to struggle with the decision to say 'yes' to the Father. It was neither simple nor sudden. But Francis gradually discovered the freedom that is ours when we commit ourselves to the God who calls. How does it feel to do that? Is it a gradual thing or does it happen all at once? Does the goal seem to change just when we think we have arrived? The words of Francis give us some answers. The life of Francis give us still other answers. They speak of his trust in God and the consequent ability to respect men. These words, written to Brother Leo, express the freedom he felt in dealing with the Brothers.

> As a mother to her child, I speak to you, my son. In this one word, this one piece of advice, I want to sum up all that we said on our journey and, in case hereafter you still find it necessary to come to me for advice, I want to say this to you: In whatever way you think you will best please our Lord God and follow in his footsteps and in poverty, take that way with the Lord God's blessing and my obedience. And if you find it necessary for your peace of soul or your own consolation and you want to come to me, Leo, then come.
> *Writings of St Francis*, Fahey-Hermann, 118 - 119

Francis is able to trust Leo's decision about God's will. Francis offers approval even before a decision is made. He is available for consultation, but does not demand it. He could respect the judgement of Brother Leo because he trusted the Father. This reflects the manner in which the heavenly Father treats us. He trustfully respects us and leaves us free in our decisions. It is his gift to us, yet he leaves us free in using it. But he is always present to help should the need arise. He is not a dictator-God but a friend-God. When we open the door of our life to him, he pours in, filling us with his own goodness and calling us to complete response.

How important is this? Ask yourself how important it is to feel trusted. Trust speaks loudly the presence of love. Love disregards the risks involved in trust and commits itself even before the fact. Such a love helps me to be trustworthy. It binds me to the friends who gave me such trust. When we realize that we are loved in this way by our Father, we are free to risk trusting others and drawing them to growth. The man who experiences such love from the Father can also reach out in forgiveness and reconciliation.

I should like you to prove that you love God and me,
his servant and yours in the following way. There should
be no friar in the whole world who has fallen into sin,
no matter how far he has fallen, who will ever fail to
find forgiveness for the asking, if he will only look into
your eyes. And if he does not ask forgiveness, you
should ask him if he wants it. And should he appear
before you again a thousand times, you should love him
more than you love me, so you may draw him to God;
you should always have pity on such friars.

Writings of St Francis, Fahey-Hermann, 110

The admonition of the Lord to forgive seventy times seven
times is not an imposition, but a way of loving. Pride can
keep a man from seeking forgiveness. Seek him out so that he
can be reconciled! The need is great. Let your love be
proportioned to the need. Such are the consequences of
following the gospel way of life. Gospel ideals and values
must touch the practical decisions that are made in life. They
must influence the manner in which we respond to human
needs and situations. The gospel in its full radiance must
shine on our lives. It will illuminate our concern for the
poor. It will touch the manner in which we approach
religious education as well as the manner in which we use our
time. It will move us to take time for prayer and dignify the
way in which we work. It must govern our choice of
recreations as well as our opinions on politics and govern-
ment. The gospel will influence our decision about what
organizations we join as well as our community involvement.
It will determine our friendship with each other and the
extent of it as well as make us aware of our need for the
sacraments. It forms the attitudes we develop about our
own bodies and our understanding of sex as well as keeping
clearsighted vision of things that might keep us from
the Father. Ours is the gospel way of life! The gospel must
touch us where we live and not simply in our discussions

about it. Francis knew that this was his way.

Our Lord Jesus Christ told his disciples: "I am the way, the truth and the life. No one comes to the Father but through me. If you had known me, you would also have known the Father. And henceforth you do know him and you have seen him." . . .

Sacred Scripture tells us that the Father dwells in 'light inaccessible' (1 Tim 6:16) and that 'God is Spirit' (John 4:24) and St John adds "No one at any time has seen God." (1:18) Because God is a spirit he can be seen only in the Spirit. 'It is the Spirit that gives life, the flesh profits nothing.' (John 6:64) But God the Son is equal to the Father and so he too can be seen only in the same way as the Father and the Holy Spirit. That is why all those are condemned who saw our Lord Jesus Christ in his humanity but did not see or believe in spirit in his divinity, that he was the true Son of God. In the same way now, all those are damned who see the sacrament of the Body of Christ which is consecrated on the altar in the form of bread and wine by the words of the Lord in the hands of the priest, and do not see or believe in spirit and in God that this is really the holy Body and Blood of our Lord Jesus Christ. It is the most High who has told us: 'This is my body and blood of the new covenant,' (Mark 14:22-24) and 'He who eats my flesh and drinks my blood has life everlasting.' (John 6:55)

And so it is really the Spirit of God who dwells in his faithful who receive the most holy Body and Blood of our Lord. Anyone who does not have this Spirit and presumes to receive him, eats and drinks judgement to himself. (1 Cor 11:29) And so we may ask in the words of Scripture: 'Men of rank, how long will you be dull

of heart?' (Ps 4:3) 'Why do you refuse to recognize the truth and believe in the Son of God?' (John 9:35)
Writings of St Francis, Fahey-Hermann, 78

Francis is filled with the living word of Scripture. But it was not just a memory exercise. For Francis the word was life. Our own personal lifestyle will reflect our integration with the word of the Lord. When we face issues, the gospel will color our attitude. About war; we cannot accept it as a solution for human problems. About life; we must fight to protect life at every level. Whether a person is only beginning life in the darkness of the womb or living life in its twilight, the gospel requires the same strong commitment to life. The right of each man to live a decent life is as vital an issue as is the issue of bombing. The dignity of marriage must be elevated as a sign of God's love present through two people as well as the loving dedication of a priest or religious must show the power of the Father's love in human lives. The Scripture requires us to control our tongue and to teach the truth. It requires us to show compassion and to be strong in standing up for the dignity of God and his Church. The Scripture requires more than an intellectual understanding of phrases from the gospel. It requires us to follow the Lord and his way no matter what the price to ourselves. We will share friendship with others as our Lord has done for us. Camus put it this way: "Don't walk in front of me; I may not follow. Don't walk behind me; I may not lead. Walk beside me and just be my friend." Franciscans accept this as part of their lifestyle.

Blessed that friar who loves his brother as much when he is sick and can be of no use to him as when he is well and can be of use to him. Blessed that friar who loves and respects his brother as much when he is absent as when he is present and who would not say anything behind his back that he could

not charitably say to his face.
Writings of St Francis, Fahey-Hermann, 86

As a partial help in understanding your own position in relation to the gospel-life, reflect on these questions. Do you find yourself putting people in categories or stereotypes and refusing to let them out? How often do you walk away from annoying people? What gospel value do you use in dealing with difficult people? Do you really try to extend yourself in serving others? Have you compressed your reach-out so that you can be comfortable? Do you love people or merely use them for your own satisfaction? Are you able to accept love from others graciously? Are you thankful to others and let them know it? Does your language reflect respect for your ability to speak? Do you hold grudges? How much time do you take to 'stand still' before God in prayer? How often do you read and reflect on the Scriptures? Are you doing any good in the organizations you belong to or are you just a hanger-on looking for the benefits? This is only a short list, but it can begin to disturb any complacency in you. Even more important, however, is what you plan to do to change things that need changing. Knowledge is fine, but it ought to lead to action if you are serious about following the gospel.

A Franciscan fraternity that is growing will have members who are changing themselves with the help of the Lord. It is sometimes difficult to keep pace with another's change. It is easier if everyone stays the same. Their change requires a change in our relationship with them. We sometimes balk at this. But from the gospel perspective this is what fraternity will always be doing. It certainly will keep us from growing stagnant and rutted. What's more, we will learn to allow our friends the freedom to grow as they can. Fraternity life ought to disturb us so that we do not get boxed in to a small world. We cannot allow ourselves the luxury of basking in the sunshine of past accomplishments. Our determination and direction is kept fresh by the creative impulse of our Father.

This side of the picture of love is attractive. Even if we are not always ready to accept the challenge of fraternity life, we can see the value of it. There is another reality about love that Jesus shows us. It is the reality of suffering. Neither Jesus nor his Father wishes to call us to suffering. Suffering is never an end to be desired. In the gospel we discover that from the moment that Jesus stayed behind in the temple at the age of 12 to his agonizing death on the cross many years later, the will of the Father was important to him. As we pilgrim after him through the pages of his gospel, he repeats, over and over again, how vital his identification with the Father is to him. "Did you not know I must be about my Father's business?" "Who is my mother and who are my brethren? Those who do the will of my Father are mother and brother and sister to me." "Father, glorify your son." "Father, if it is possible, take this cup from me; yet, not my will but yours be done." "Father, forgive them for they know not what they do." "Father, into your hands I commend my spirit." There is something special here. Not just words about a far off, unknown God. Jesus speaks of his Father with such love that he could not be himself without his relationship with the Father. All the evidence of the gospels point to this close union. The prayer of Jesus at the Last Supper confirms this closeness, for Jesus prays for the same closeness and unity for us.

If we see it rightly, then, we can come to the passion and death of Jesus to find the answer for suffering. But our human vision is still hard put to understand. Jesus is responsive to the Father right to the end. He willingly embraces the suffering of the cross if the Father so wills. Yet when crucifixion becomes a reality, it seems that the Father is silent. Jesus cries out in agony: "My God, my God, why have you forsaken me?" It is a difficult moment in our Christian reflection. Why was the Father silent at this point of great need? For three days that question is impossible to answer. Death has triumphed; the apostles are disheartened and afraid; Christian development seems to have come to a crunching halt on a hill outside Jerusalem known as Calvary. The answer comes on that first day of the week when the tomb is discovered to be empty. "He is risen! He is not here!" In the rays of the first Easter dawn we are able finally to understand Good Friday. In all the agony and suffering; through each moment of seeming defeat; in Jesus' clinging to the Father despite all human agony and seeming abandonment; through it all the will of the Father looked to the moment of glorification and life. His will had seen this moment. He desired life for his Son all along.

> The message of the cross is complete absurdity to those who are headed for ruin, but to us who are experiencing salvation, it is the power of God . . . Where is the wise man to be found? Where the Scribe? Where is the master of worldly argument? Has not God turned the wisdom of this world into folly? Since in God's wisdom the world did not come to know him through 'wisdom,' it pleased God to save those who believe through the absurdity of the preaching of the gospel. Yes, Jews demand 'signs,' and Greeks look for 'wisdom,' but we preach Christ crucified—a stumbling block to Jews, and an absurdity to the Gentiles; but to those who are called, Jews and Greeks alike, Christ, the power and wisdom of God. For God's folly is wiser than men and his weakness more powerful than men.
>
> 1 Corinthians 1: 18 - 25

At the very roots of suffering is the possibility of a love so deep that nothing can destroy it. Suffering reveals a love that is full of a sense of giving with no hope of return. Its value is not in some stoical, passive resignation to inevitable events. Its value lies in the ability of total love to actively embrace the cross in order to reach life. In imitation of

Jesus we kneel freely before our Father and embrace his gift of suffering. The agony of arrest, scourging, abandonment by friends and eventual crucifixion and death were not embraced for their own sake. Jesus chose to accept these things freely so that he might remain one with the Father. Everything seemed to militate against this kind of acceptance, yet it is a way to maintain union with the Father. The gospel answers the question of suffering by speaking clearly of the consequences of friendship with the Father. We are no longer servants, but friends. Friends do not abandon friendship in the face of trial. As Father and Son were more deeply united through the work of those few days so many years ago, so we will come to life if our free acceptance bonds us to the Father no matter what demands he may make.

> May the power of your love, o Lord, fiery, and sweet as honey, wean my heart from all that is under heaven, so that I may die for love of your love, you who were so good to die for love of my love.
>   *Writings of St Francis*, Fahey-Hermann, 161

Francis understood the burning love in the heart of Jesus. Love is God's name. Francis and Franciscans will always bless that name and follow wherever it calls, even through the valley of darkness and pain.

> May I never boast of anything but the cross of our Lord Jesus Christ! Through it, the world has been crucified to me and I to the world. It means nothing whether one is circumcised or not. All that matters is that one is created anew. Peace and mercy on all who follow this rule of life . . .
>   Galatians 6: 14 - 16

As with everything else in his life, Francis embraced the cross with an enthusiasm and joy that showed the strength of his faith. It was a positive, active acceptance of this way to life. Love does such things. Those who do not know how to love will not be able to understand. But it is the way to shalom and integrity.

Our own understanding will grow as we experience the qualities of real love. When we can begin to face a friend's cancer with the gift of our faith and love. When we can face our personal loss of good friends through misunderstanding with the calmness of acceptance based on faith and continued love. When our life seems empty and the good things we do no longer satisfy us, this faith in the Father will lead us to continued love for him. No matter how puzzling and unexplainable the will of the Father may seem, Francis and Jesus call us to say 'yes' in faith from a heart that seems empty. The form of our own passion is unique to ourselves. But the Father is not looking at the passion but to the resurrection he calls us to experience. The prayer of St Francis makes sense now, for it speaks of his deep commitment to being one with Jesus.

> Lord Jesus Christ, I entreat you to give me two graces before I die. First, that in my lifetime I may feel in body and soul, as far as possible, the pain you endured, dear Lord, in the hour of your most bitter suffering; and second, that I may feel in my heart, as far as possible, that excess of love by which you, O Son of God, were inflamed to undertake so cruel a suffering for us sinners.
>
> *Words of St Francis*, 16

The way to the Father is the way of Jesus. There are no magic short-cuts, no instant ways to holiness. Only the way of Jesus. No one else. No other way. Francis tries to proclaim this fact by his gospel way of life. The Word-made-flesh walked the slopes of both Tabor and Calvary, and He is the way. The Word-made-flesh agonized in responding to the

Father yet freely chose to accept the Father's will, and He is the way. Crucifixion and death followed this free response, and Jesus is the way. Finally, on the first day of the week, the Word-made-flesh rose from the dead to new life, and He is the way.

> I have been crucified with Christ, and the life I now live is not my own; Christ is living in me. I still live my human life, but it is a life of faith in the Son of God, who loved me and gave himself for me. I will not treat God's gracious gift as pointless.
>
> Galatians 2: 20 - 21

Today, then, when you reflect on the ways of love, reflect on the life of Jesus. Today, then, when you see all the bumper stickers about love and hear all the tunes about love and all the cliches about love, remember the way of Jesus. Today, then, when the Father calls you to accept a share of the cross of his son, remember that it is the way to life. Today, when you rise from your prayer to deal with life as it comes to you this day, know that you are loved as totally today as our Father can love you. Know hope in that love and know that you can praise the Father for his own sake. Sing out your praise to the Lord as did Francis in his beautiful canticle to Brother Sun, calling on all of creation to praise the Lord. Brother Sun, Sister moon and stars, Brother Fire and Sister earth, even Sister Death, Come and praise the Lord. Praise and bless my lord and give him thanks and serve him with great humility.

12. Come to Me

OUR WORLD HAS A VARIETY OF SIGNS. Highway signs that used to contain a lot of words are giving way to 'symbol' signs so that anyone can 'read' them. The style of clothes can be a sign of a particular lifestyle. Trademarks on a can of soup reveals the company that produces it. Signs and symbols are serious ways of communicating.

The signs and symbols of life are also used in the framework of our faith. In his preaching our Lord often used illustrations from life to signify his meaning. Walking through the countryside and seeing the grape arbors gave rise to his speaking of himself as the vine and all of us as the branches. The shepherds who tended flocks were often among his listeners. So he would often speak about being a good shepherd or seeking out a sheep that is lost. Taking signs and tasks that were familiar to his listeners, he led them to a fuller understanding of his message. They served as signs and illustrations for his word of life. Jesus took advantage of the things around him and used them to help people understand his message. The sacramental system is the beneficiary of this action of the Lord. Here too we have signs and symbols that point to a deeper reality.

The sacraments do not use signs and symbols by accident. The signs have meaning and serve to indicate the presence of Jesus. They are signs taken from life. It is Jesus' way of saying to us through this sign-language: "Here I am, come to Me." The Sacraments span the centuries and put us in touch with Jesus. They are meeting places with the savior. Each sacrament touches a corner of life that needs salvation and healing and strengthening from the Lord. He gives us life and reconciles us to himself and to each other; he nourishes us through the intimacy of communion and praises his Father through our worship; he walks with the couple who commit themselves to one another and is the ever-present strength for his priestly minister; he comes in time of sickness to share our loneliness and sends his Spirit to strengthen us in our weakness. For each contact point there is a sign of his presence.

The sacraments are signs of the presence of Jesus for special points in our lives as Christians. It is the way that Jesus has chosen to say: "I love you and I am here for you." Unlike ordinary signs which depend on us to fulfill their meaning, the sacramental signs say clearly and distinctly that Jesus is here.

What difference does this make for our lives? In a day and age when we are faced with monumental problems in society; when we are faced with a Third World on the brink of starvation and restlessness; when the cloud of suspicion and distrust seem to cover relations between nations and people; when we have more loneliness than ever before even while we face a problem of population that is not easy to deal with; when within the Church there are voices at such far ends of the spectrum of opinion that it is difficult to see how we are still united: in the face of all of this, what do the sacraments have to offer?

The science editor of a metropolitan newspaper takes a hard look at some of these problems and examines their implications for people. Looking ahead, he labels the future as an age of depression. Uncertainty, loneliness, social isolation and frustration have led to more and more depression. Escape from all this takes the form of suicide, drugs, alcohol, withdrawal and non-involvement, following every new fantasy and fanaticism that come along, from devil-worship to violence as a vehicle of change. Apathy, fear, cruelty to others are a part of the parade of symptoms. People feel helpless in the face of problems far beyond their ability to solve. The human person needs more knowledge and understanding in order to deal with the material universe around him and the technology that grows up in a hundred directions. People need friends. We need other people who really care about us and help us realize our worth. People need to believe in something that gives meaning to life. Perhaps we need someone to believe in so that we can find meaning for life. This editor is saying that we need to know and deal with the knowledge explosion around us so that our minds are nourished and can function. We need a community that cares about us so that we can escape the loneliness and isolation we so often feel. We need to believe that life is worth living and that there is meaning to life.

Jesus has offered us a possibility of fulfillment on all three counts. He has given to men the responsibility for creation. We are the rulers of creation and it is our responsibility to use it wisely. It is meant to be a help and a reminder of the goodness of the Father. Jesus has established a community of believers, his Church, as a group of friends united with himself. He is the one who offers us himself to believe in. He reveals his truth and life to us through the Scriptures and the power of his Spirit at work. He calls us to life and shows us that even death cannot strip us of his life. The life and message of Jesus brings us the things we need to face life today and to move with hope to our future. But it requires faith in Jesus that is real and personal. Without it, we too can join in the chorus of doomsday people. However, Franciscans are expected to be a people of faith, facing tomorrow with hope because of Jesus Christ.

Throughout our lives Jesus touches us in what we might call the high points and need-points of life. His power is present to be our strength when we are weak. We are called to love one another and he is present in the sign of intimacy to teach us how and to walk with us on the way. He calls us to reconciliation with God, with ourselves, with other people and with creation and he is present then to forgive and to lead and to bring us to the Father. But his way will lead to light and joy only if we lose ourselves in him. When we seek self-satisfaction we shall find only darkness and despair. When we leave behind self-seeking, we shall walk in the light that is Christ. We shall seek and search, we shall question and explore when we walk in the light. But we shall not fear the questions for Jesus is the truth and the truth will make us free. Or we can clutter our lives with things that are ultimately unimportant and be confused by our own stupid seeking of non-essentials. We can use questioning as an escape from being, or mistake the ways and means for the goal. All such things lead to darkness and aloneness. When we seek the Lord with an open heart and freely abandon ourselves to Him, we become sharers of good news, news that Christ is alive and well and loving us with all his heart. The sacraments call us in faith to remember that he is present for us. They are signs of hope when we slip into hopelessness; signs of love when we feel abandoned.

The sacraments are not magical cures for all our ills. Rather, they are points of contact with the living Jesus who can lead me beyond myself and self-seeking to his kind of creative love. I need that! The sacramental encounters with Jesus are not frills on the fringes of faith, to be used when I feel like it. They are intimate and essential elements of real faith for they are the actions of Jesus reaching out to touch my life. The sacraments are meeting places with Jesus and through him with the Father. We listen intently to the message of the signs so that we might understand the meaning Jesus wants to communicate to us.

> This is what we proclaim to you; what was from the beginning, what we have heard, what we have seen with our eyes, what we have looked upon and our hands have touched—we speak of the word of life.

(This life became visible; we have seen and bear witness
to it, and we proclaim to you the eternal life that was
present to the Father and became visible to us.) What
we have seen and heard we proclaim in turn to you so
that you may share life with us. This fellowship of ours
is with the Father and with his Son, Jesus Christ.
Indeed, our purpose in writing you this is that our joy
may be complete.

Here, then, is the message we have heard from him and
announce to you: That God is light; in him there is no
darkness.

1 John 1: 1 - 5

When communication is really working, it is a two-way
thing. Since the sacramental contacts with Jesus are times of
personal communing, we must not only speak to the Lord
but listen to him as well. We come in faith to a point of
contact that is meant to strengthen us in our faith and move
us to hope and love.

The sacraments are Christ's body reaching out to us for
us to see, touch, hear, receive, and let ourselves be
transformed into him and by him.

Credo, Louis Evely, 110

Friends influence one another. The sacraments of Jesus
are meant to influence our way of life. The reconciliation of
penance should move us to change our sinfulness into a
stronger seeking of virtue. The intimacy of Eucharist ought
to move us to identify more clearly with Jesus of Nazareth
in our ideas and attitudes and lifestyle. Each sacrament calls
for a deepening of friendship and a more open readiness to
be influenced by Jesus.

When we reflect on the passion, death and resurrection of
Jesus, we might conclude that his presence on earth was

over with his ascension into heaven. But such is not the case. Jesus is with us. He has given us words and signs that speak of his presence. In his glorified, human body, he is no longer limited by the barriers of time and place. He is free to be present wherever he chooses. He is present in many different ways. He is present through his intimacy with people who are poor and in need. He is present in his word in the Scriptures, speaking his message to us through that living word. His presence in the sacramental sign is a special meeting place. Jesus is human still, but that human nature is now glorified and stripped of any earthly limitation. He is now present wherever the signs of his presence are repeated. He is present in this century of ours, in our town and in our lives, here and now, to relate to us.

> To accomplish so great a work (salvation), Christ is always present in his Church, especially in her liturgical celebrations. He is present in the sacrifice of the Mass, not only in the person of the minister, "the same now offering, through the ministry of priests, who formerly offered himself on the cross," but especially under the Eucharistic species. By his power he is present in the Sacraments, so that when a man baptizes it is really Christ himself who baptizes. He is present in his word, since it is he himself who speaks when the holy Scriptures are read in Church. He is present, lastly, when the Church prays and sings, for he promised: 'Where two or three are gathered in my name, there am I in the midst of them.' (Mt 18:20)
>
> *Constitution on the Sacred Liturgy*, #7

We grow in our relationship to Jesus in the same way that all friendships grow. The sacraments are places where friends meet. Friends influence one another. The way in which Jesus views things, the attitude he reveals in the gospel, the readiness to help and his availability, all speak loudly to us about our own attitudes and readiness to help. If our reception of the sacraments is truly a faith-encounter with the living Jesus, it will touch our lives. No magic is involved, only the care and concern of Jesus for his people. Our contact with Jesus in the sacraments requires us to live like friends of his. The influence of Jesus (grace) will touch us only if we are responsive and receptive and aware of our need to meet him in faith. Going through the motions without any real commitment to friendship with Jesus will be good for nothing. The gospel-contacts where Jesus touched the lives of different people are filled with the demand of Jesus to be different and better. His forgiveness was joined to a call to sin no more. His healing called for a deeper faith. All of this means that when we walk away from the contact point of the sacrament, we remain friends of Jesus, and we are expected to live accordingly. A husband is not a husband only when he and his wife are together. He is always her husband and is expected to act according to that relationship. He cannot play act at being a husband and expect his love relationship to grow. Being a husband is part of the reality of being himself. The same is true of our friendship with Jesus. The reality of being ourselves is tied, in faith, to our friendship with the Lord.

Among the important qualities that we will need we might consider the following. We need to have the will and desire to belong to Jesus. This is a matter of choosing Jesus and accepting all the consequences of such a choice. We need to be open to change and conversion. Jesus will always call us to deeper friendship and that will require moving in the direction he calls us to move. Responsive listening may sometimes be painful for us. We may not always like to hear the gospel. But openness to Jesus is vital for our growth in the Spirit. We must be ready to forgive those who have hurt us in any way. Bitterness and resentment that go unresolved are dangerous diseases that sap faith-life. To refuse to forgive or to harbor and nourish anger and jealousy and hatred and resentment, is to paralyze our growth in the Spirit. We will need to grow in our trust of the Lord and grow in our trustworthiness. I cannot go on excusing myself when I need to change some habit or attitude. Life is the proving ground of trust and trustworthiness. It is the preparation ground for our encounter with Jesus in the sacraments. No magical concepts or miraculous actions will change us without effort. But when we are responsive the power of the Spirit can do things that we could not have imagined.

The sacraments are normal necessities for a good Christian life. No intimacy can long survive absence. Our Fraternity-community must sink its roots deeply into the gospel of Jesus. We will be a community going again and again to the source of all life, Jesus himself. It would be nothing less than foolishness for Franciscans to neglect the sacraments. But it would be more than foolish to think that they shall magically transform us or that they are some sort of sugar pill to satisfy our cravings. Contact with Jesus in the sacraments as well as any other contact with Jesus, will require us to move toward handing over the whole of our lives to him. No one who wants to hang on to the 'things' that hold him back is ready for the fullness of the kingdom of God. Above all, the Lord wants us to have wholeness and total integrity. His gospel, his sacraments, his Church, all call us to follow Jesus and leave everything else behind. Then we are free to use the things of the world for their real purpose, to bring us to the Father.

When we become one with the Father, then we too will become sacraments. We shall be signs to the world of hope and faith. We shall not fear what knowledge brings us, for when we come to the truth we shall find that its name is Jesus. We shall not run from the problems of loneliness and boredom, but rather be free to follow the gospel way of life for it too shall bring us to one who is the way, Jesus. Finally, when we are able to be more generous in handing over the whole of ourselves to the way of the gospel, we shall find life itself, and his name is Jesus. Then we shall be the signs of his presence in the world, for we shall reflect his love of the Father and be a sign of hope for those in darkness, for we shall live in the light. And the name of the light is Jesus.

13. Call on Me

TWO SACRAMENTS ARE OF SPECIAL IMPORTANCE in the life of the Christian, namely, the Eucharist and the sacrament of reconciliation. Writing in his letter to all the Faithful, St Francis says this:

> And moreover, we should confess all our sins to a priest and receive from him the Body and Blood of our Lord Jesus Christ. The man who doesn't eat his flesh and drink his blood cannot enter into the kingdom of God. (John 6:54) Only he must eat and drink worthily because he who eats and drinks unworthily without distinguishing the Body, eats and drinks judgement to himself. (1 Cor 11:29)

> Besides this, we must bring forth fruits befitting repentance (Luke 3:8) and love our neighbor as ourselves. Anyone who will not or cannot love his neighbor as himself should at least do him good and not do him any harm.
>
> *Writings of St Francis*, Fahey-Hermann, 94

In his ministry, Jesus was often in touch with people who had sinned. Sins of prostitution, adultery, misuse of sacred things, lies, betrayal, lack of faith, the 'big lie' technique of the authorities who wanted him out of the way. Throughout his life Jesus experienced contact with the power of evil. Likewise we are given a clear picture of Jesus' reaction to sin and sin situations. He often made it clear that the sin was not just something to be shrugged off or forgotten as of no account. He dealt with the reality of sin directly and sought to remove this barrier from the lives of people. He recognized the guilt of sin and the need for forgiveness and healing. "I forgive you your sins," "Go now and sin no more" are regular in the response of Jesus. In terms of friendship, sin becomes that action or attitude or refusal to act that keeps a person from deeper intimacy and/or drives a person away from the way to Jesus. Temptation is something we all face as Jesus himself experienced in the desert. The temptation to gain power; the temptation to get something for nothing; the temptation to acclaim and glory without having to earn it; these are things we all experience. The reality of sin needs no proving. The reality of our own weakness is taught by personal experience. The need to be forgiven and healed is a clear need for people who have faith in God and know how often God's call to greatness is rejected. Our relationship with Jesus often suffers from our mediocrity in responding to Him. Sin often blocks total generosity in us. We experience the effects of self-seeking that diminishes our sensitiveness to the call of the Spirit. All of these kinds of things point to a need to come to Jesus for forgiveness and healing. As a gospel people, Franciscans become more and more aware of the fact that the gospel is a disturbing thing. As we grow to a deeper awareness of the word of God, we also sense more clearly the gap between what the gospel requires and what we actually do. Again, we stand in need of a contact point with Jesus in order to be strengthened and healed for giving a more complete response. The sacrament of reconciliation is that point. Here is where our friendship with Jesus is made more stable because he directly forgives our sins and touches us with his healing compassion.

But this sacrament of reconciliation may leave us in somewhat of a puzzlement. Like anything else it can become a routine and patterned thing. We may find that we repeat the same sort of sins every time. It may seem to us that nothing much happens through this sacrament and little by little we drift away from it. What is meant to be an encounter of healing and forgiveness and strength can become something mundane and seemingly useless.

Some distinctions are in order here. First of all, this sacrament may be either obligatory or reflective (devotional). In the first case we speak of the 'obligation' of confession when a mortal sin has separated us from Jesus. In such a case, this contact with Jesus is essential for us, it is an obligation. Anyone who is certain, in his conscience, that he is guilty of mortal sin, should go to confession before receiving the Eucharist. Anyone who is certain, in his conscience, that he is guilty of mortal sin, should go to confession at least once within the year. These are two traditional rules of the Church. Now 'mortal' sin means that a person intentionally directs the whole thrust of his life away from the love of God and neighbor and builds a wall between himself and God and/or neighbor. Such an action, done with sufficient reflection and full intent, is considered a rupture in the friendship with the Lord. If such a person wishes to restore the relationship and turn back to God and neighbor, he should seek the sacramental sign of forgiveness and reconciliation.

Such a total turning from God may be rare in the life of a concerned Christian. But we all experience times when our personal guilt and personal failures or some of the things we say or do began to cripple us in our relationship with Jesus. We lose some of the zest for following the gospel. We turn more and more to questioning the value of faith or prayer or some particular practice the gospel calls for. We become a bit more concerned about our own image or 'getting ahead' than we are about our neighbor's welfare. We still love God and neighbor, but we show it less and more easily find excuses for ourselves when the gospel appears a bit too tough. Such a crippling experience is not rare. It is all too common.

There are many ways to begin to deal with this experience. One very powerful one is to come to Jesus in the sacrament of reconciliation to be touched by his forgiveness and understanding and strengthened by his healing. In such a contact, we try to get to the sources and roots of our sins rather than simply listing our sins. We sense that our drift into indifference may spring from a lack of faith and so we explore the depth of our faith. Or our anger and irritability with others may reveal a self-centered attitude that needs change. We come to Jesus for forgiveness and help in the sacrament of reconciliation.

This sacramental encounter than becomes something more than a making-up place for a total break. It is rather a meeting with Jesus to talk over where we are on the way to him. It is a coming to him to share our need to be forgiven and understood and to know the healing power of his sacramental word. There is no arrogance here; no fooling ourselves about how good we are. Rather, there is an honest, responsible awareness that the call of the gospel does not always find a receptive welcome in our lives. There is an awareness that we cannot settle a firm direction in our lives without the strength of Jesus. It tells Jesus of our own sensitive conscience that still is growing in its awareness of how easy it is to fail and how difficult to love as Jesus does and to be perfect as is the Father.

We might do well to call to mind here that the actual confession of our sins to the priest is only one part of an ongoing process. The process of conversion does not take place only in confession. Neither is the sacramental action simply narrowed to the few moments of contact between priest and penitent. Rather, actual confession is a part of the sweep of actions that keeps leading me to conversion and new life. The particular action of confession is a high point in the manifestation of God's love for us and elicits another dedicated response in us. At issue in this sacramental action is my personal awareness of the need not only for forgiveness, but for conversion; not only to say words but to change my way of life and be reconciled with God and neighbor. Ongoing conversion ought to result from this contact with the Lord. He looks for and anticipates a fresh start in us through the power of his Spirit.

The history of penance gives us some insight into the meaning of this sacrament in the life of the Church. Our Lord dealt often with the sinner. One of the things that comes clear in the gospel is that the acceptance Jesus gave the sinner was often an impetus to change. Zaccheus, the little man in the sycamore tree, did a whole about-face when Jesus simply accepted him by asking to dine with Zaccheus. Zaccheus starts fresh and makes restitution even though Jesus said nothing about it. The woman caught in adultery is forgiven rather than condemned, but Jesus also asks those who caught her in sinning to look at themselves. "He who is without sin, cast the first stone." Again, the parable of the good father (sometimes called the parable of the Prodigal Son) illustrates the acceptance our Father gives if we show even an ounce of willingness to change. The Father in the story had every right to wait until the son came begging at his doorstep. But when he saw his son 'a long way off' he already moves toward him to show forgiveness. Our heavenly Father is like that. This is the acceptance that helps us to change. But it is not easy for us to do that when we are hurt. So we find it hard to accept Jesus' attitude toward us as being so forgiving. It seems unreal; too much to hope for. Yet it *is* real and we can hope for it. The early church was deeply aware that the community of believers played an important part in helping the sinner come to repentance by its attitude of acceptance. It means that our own personal attitudes and opinions have something to do with the way that a sinner will feel supported in his conversion or turned away by a prejudiced look and approach. The manner in which the sacrament is understood will make a difference in our own response as well. If confession of sins is all there is to penance, then it can too easily become a place to 'dump' our sins so that we can be forgiven. Should such a narrow concept continue, we would probably never experience the wholeness the total sacramental action is meant to have. Jesus forgives in order to free us for more complete service to him and to our neighbor by using our gifts of time and life in a more loving and responsive way. The revised rite of confession gives various ways of approaching confession and shows the different ways in which we need to sense the presence of God in our lives. To be touched by the priest, to have him lay his hands on us, is a reminder that this is a place of healing for the sinner. To share with the confessor a time to reflect on the Scriptures will mean that we look to the foundation stone of our Christian lives to see how we fulfill the gospel. In short, each rite of the sacramental encounter speaks loudly to the Franciscan and to every Christian of the vitality of the relationship of Christ and Christian.

We will find that this ongoing process of real penance (conversion - metanoia) needs Jesus if it is to continue. Fraternity life will require things of us that we are not always ready to give. Reconciliation will be a constant need in this group of people. Reconciliation with God, reconciliation with one's self, with neighbor and with all of creation. We are little brothers, in constant need of reconciliation and renewal. Faith speaks loudly that Jesus is present to help us in this growth. We will be able to reach the impossible dream of Francis and Christ because we are a people of faith. We are a poor people, ready to hand ourselves over to the Lord. No longer will we run from accepting responsibility for our failings. No more will we excuse and rationalize and blame others. We shall take a mature look at ourselves and compare that look with the demands of the gospel. We will know our need for a savior; our need for forgiveness; our need for the living Jesus to be our companion and strength and our need of an accepting community to help us move past failure to embracing the way of Jesus. We know, that without Jesus, we can do nothing!

There are many forms of 'half-truth' that we use to escape honest evaluation of our lives. Pride can be a source either of solid and sound acceptance of self or an artificial, put-on sort of thing that is dishonest. When pride becomes arrogant and independent of God, it is a hindrance to friendship with Jesus. Sometimes it shows itself by a refusal to seek help when help is needed. We 'bull our way through' because we are too proud to face the reality of our need for help. If we are consistently that way, we become opinionated, dogmatic, and a darn nuisance to others. Not only does our friendship with Jesus suffer, but the community of people around us also suffers. Other people have a pride that expresses itself by never deciding until you ask a whole host of people about something. What often occurs in this instance is that there will be disagreement among those asked. Now you can do what you want since nobody agrees on what to do. It is a clever way to get your own way because it really looks so wise. Some people always blame others for mistakes. Anything that goes wrong is the other fellow's fault. Then there is the person who condemns others who try to develop programs and projects. Since nothing human is going to be perfect, this character never runs out of things to condemn. Of course, he never does anything either! Since all of the above mentioned people are so 'righteous,' they obviously feel no need for confession.

Selfishness is also a hindrance to growth in Christ. The selfish person almost unconsciously does everything to make certain that he gets what he wants. Should he have his day planned and scheduled, he cannot possibly be bothered by a need that would upset his schedule. Should he be busy enjoying his leisure, he certainly cannot be called away should someone need his assistance. Or, should he condescend to help, everyone will know of the great sacrifices he made to give his help. The selfish person uses people.

Husband or wife are accepted so long as he or she fulfills the desires that arise in oneself. A friend is of worth only if he always agrees and goes along with the selfish person. Organizations are all right as long as they don't get too demanding. The Church is OK so long as she doesn't expect the selfish one to change or do much by way of participation. There is only one #1 in the book of the selfish person, and that #1 is always taken care of first.

The vain person also has problems in relationships. Often he is so concerned with his 'image' that anything will be done to promote that image. He has to look good no matter who may suffer as a result. The latest styles, the 'in' language and styles, the attention-drawing actions and attitudes all contribute to this image. They may be nothing but a big front, but they are more important than being real. The trouble is, God knows the heart of each of us, and all the play-acting in the world will not fool him. Sometimes people use simplistic cliches as the way of finding God. Beautiful, nice-sounding and platitudinous words flow like lava from their mouths. "Love everyone and all will be well." "What difference what I believe, we all get to God anyway." "I take my sins direct to God without all this in-between business." "Trust everybody." "The Spirit will solve it." Every one of these sayings has seeds of truth. But for some they become mere mouthings that sound good but never demand anything. It is the 'talking game' of holiness that avoids the cross.

The person who truly does not or says he cannot forgive another is also in trouble. Bitterness, resentment, jealousy, refusal to forgive someone, all of these things serve to destroy the person who is possessed by them. They are not gospel qualities, yet there are people who wish to be gospel-people who refuse to forgive; who refuse to be reconciled. Such people will never be healed by the sacrament of Penance for there is no soil for the good seed of compassion and understanding to grow. Only when we let loose of such negative things can we grow again. The point here is not that 'feelings' such as these exist, but that we make no decision to move away from allowing these feelings to direct our lives. We are not always able to dismiss feelings. But we can decide to forgive and take the actions of forgiveness and reconciliation. We are guilty when we refuse to decide, not simply because we have the feelings. Again, not to decide for reconciliation is to decide against it. That is the tragedy and that is the obstacle to growth.

Scrupulosity is another most painful deception. It might even be called a neurosis, for it is an unreasonable concentration on sin and an impossible sense of responsibility. The scrupulous person finds sin everywhere in his life. His morbid self-examination is a never ending agony that goes on and on and on. Whether there is really sin present or not, the scrupulant finds 'sins' present. In reality, there is a denial of Christ's power to forgive, for the scrupulant is never satisfied with his confession. It too goes on and on and on into every little detail of possible or maybe or perhaps. Even here there is pride at work, for the constant self-examination blinds the scrupulant to the needs of others and can even paralyze him to a point of inaction.

Sensitive awareness of real failure and sin is the sign of a true Christian. As we compare what we hear in the gospel and what we do in our lives, we become more aware of the gap between the two. We work hard to fill that gap. This kind of sensitive growth is to be sought prayerfully. But the scrupulant lives in an unreal world of created sins. He will need to move to trust in God and less concentration on self as he moves to the healing of the sacrament of reconciliation.

God constantly calls us to put his riches to work in our lives. He provides opportunity for sharing with others. Again and again he asks for another 'yes' to what he wants of us. Christian morality is saying 'yes' to all the gifts of God and using them with reverence and responsibility and respect. It is 'yes' to the good use of food, money, sex, sports, mind, heart, lips, time and everything that is part of life. It is 'yes' to the values of the gospel; to justice, mercy, compassion, understanding, forgiveness, poverty of spirit, acceptance of the cross, patience, faith, hope and love. When we sin, we say "No!" to all of this.

> His sins, whatever they are, have damaged his relations with God's people. His refusal to love has weakened the life-force of the Body of Christ. He has discouraged others, has given a countersign of selfishness instead of godliness, has made the Church less holy and attractive. Any mortal sins would have excluded him from the Eucharist, the sign and source of Church unity and the food necessary for healthy Christian growth.
>
> *I Confess*, Francis Buckley S.J., 12

As we allow the sacramental action of reconciliation to take root in our lives, we experience again and again the need for conversion and renewal, for change and greater generosity. The sign that the sacrament of reconciliation is at work will show in the manner in which our lives become more gentle and aware. It will show in a more generous acceptance of the will of our Father. It will show in a more ready forgiveness of enemies and a gentle acceptance of the people in our lives.

> In short, the Sacrament of Penance is a rescue operation, by which God frees man from loneliness, isolation, weakness, ignorance and fear—from radical sinfulness which lies behind particular sins and is reinforced by the cumulative effects of sins. God saves the sinner from himself and restores him to the Church, where in an atmosphere of security, acceptance and love, man can grow to the full stature of Christ.
>
> *I Confess*, Francis Buckley S.J., 16 - 17

As men and women called to follow the gospel way of Francis, we positively seek the good that is possible for us. We turn from sin in order to be free in seeking Jesus. We not only wish to rid our lives of sin, but to embrace the more important thing, responsiveness to the Spirit. We need to act in ways that reveal the gospel through our lives as well as reading the word of the gospel. The Third Order is called the Order of Penance and so it ought to be. Each of us is constantly caught up in the need for constant conversion and growth. We are called to empty ourselves, to die to ourselves, so that the Spirit might fill us.

But those things I used to consider gain I have now reappraised as loss in the light of Christ. I have come to rate all as loss in the light of the surpassing knowledge of my Lord Jesus Christ. For his sake I have forfeited everything; I have accounted all else rubbish so that Christ may be my wealth and I may be in him, not having any justice of my own based on observance of the law. The justice I possess is that which comes through faith in Christ. It has its origin in God and is based on faith. I wish to know Christ and the power flowing from his resurrection; likewise to know how to share in his sufferings by being formed into the pattern of his death. Thus do I hope that I may arrive at resurrection from the dead.

It is not that I have reached it yet, or have already finished my course; but I am racing to grasp the prize if possible, since I have been grasped by Christ Jesus. Brothers, I do not think of myself as having reached the finish line. I give no thought to what lies behind but push on to what is ahead. My entire attention is on the finish line as I run toward the prize to which God calls me—life on high in Christ Jesus.

Philippians 3: 7 - 14

EUCHARIST

At the heart of our belief is the man-God, Jesus Christ. On our relationship with him hinges our whole growth as Christians. Among all the encounters that the sacramental system offers us, none can surpass the value and necessity of the Eucharist. It is not a matter of magic. Coming to Jesus in the intimacy of communion requires a solid, daily relationship of faith and surrender. But the Eucharist will be at the very core of continued and solid growth.

> Before men can come to the liturgy, they must be called to faith and conversion . . . To believers also the Church must preach faith and penance; she must prepare them for the sacraments, teach them to observe all that Christ commanded, and invite them to all the works of charity, piety and the apostolate.
>
> Nevertheless, the liturgy is the summit toward which the activity of the Church is directed, at the same time it is the fount from which all her power flows. For the aim and object of apostolic works is that all who are made Sons of God by faith and baptism, should come together to praise God in the midst of his Church, to take part in the sacrifice and to eat the Lord's supper.
>
> *Constitution on the Sacred Liturgy*, #9 - 10

When we come to the Mass, we bring our lives and all that God has given us. From the Mass we receive the power to be more dedicated and responsive to Jesus and his gospel. At Mass, that action of salvation that happened once and for all on Calvary comes present to us here and now. The action of a loving and obedient Jesus is brought to us in all its fullness, captured forever in the timelessness that is eternity. This is the heart of the Christian life. Nothing can replace it. The Eucharist is Christ, alive and real, present to us to draw us to himself.

Of course, we are not always prepared for such intimacy. We often come to Jesus with personal and communal hang-ups. We are not always ready to celebrate and praise the presence of Jesus. We sometimes expect to be magically transformed and are filled with disappointment when there is no magic. Yet, the inner transformation of our lives will continue as we come again and again to the intimacy of Christ's presence in Eucharist. Little by little we shall be emptied out and he shall fill us, if we come in faith and surrender to this meeting place. To the Eucharist we bring all the work and play, the pain and joy, the love and suspicion, the sensitiveness and insensitivity of Christians joined in community. At Eucharist the Lord seeks to actualize us so that we are more fully alive as Christians.

> We are Christians because through the Christian community we have met Jesus Christ, heard his word of invitation and responded to him in faith. We assemble together at Mass in order to speak our faith over again in community, and by speaking it, to renew and deepen it. We do not come together to meet Christ as if he were absent from the rest of our lives. We come together to deepen our awareness of, and commitment to, the action of the Spirit in the whole of our lives at every moment. We come together to acknowledge the work of the Spirit in us, to offer thanks, to celebrate.

> People in love make signs of love and celebrate their love for the dual purpose of expressing and deepening that love. We too must express in signs, our faith in Christ and each other, our love for Christ and each other, or they will die. We need to celebrate.

> We may not feel like celebrating on this or that Sunday, even though we are called by the Church's law to do so.

Our faith does not always permeate our feelings. But this is the function of signs in the church: To give bodily expression to faith, to transform our fragile awareness of Christ's presence in the dark of our daily isolation into a joyful, integral experience of his liberating action in the solidarity of the celebrating community.

"The place of music in Eucharistic Celebrations",
Bishops' Liturgical Committee, 1968

St Francis expressed himself clearly and directly on the Eucharist. His reverence for the Eucharist, his heartfelt relationship to Jesus speaks loud and clear in his words:

So I entreat you all, with a kiss for your feet and whatever charity I can, to bring all reverence and all the respect you ever can to bear on the most holy Body and Blood of our Lord Jesus Christ, through whom whatever there is in heaven and on earth has been appeased and reconciled to Almighty God.

Words of St Francis, #192b

Let everything in man halt in awe, let all the world quake, and let the heavens exult when Christ, the son of the living God, is there on the altar in the hands of the priest! Oh admirable dignity and amazing condescension! Oh sublime lowliness! Oh, lowly sublimity! That the Lord of the universe, God and the Son of God, should so humble himself as to hide under the tiny little form of bread for our welfare. Look, Brothers, at the humility of God and pour your hearts out before him.

. . . So, do not keep anything about you back for yourselves, so that he may have you altogether as his own who puts himself altogether at your disposal.

Words of St Francis, 192e

In the course of time we have accentuated different ways of explaining the Mass. We might summarize them in three ways. First, we have understood the Mass to be a sacrifice, a 'making-present' of the death of the Lord which occurred on Calvary. It brought to our altars the saving action of Christ in dying for us. Our own lives have seen in this a very vital part of the Mass. We sense a frustration when this element of the Mass is passed over or neglected. The Mass as sacrifice and re-presentation of the action of Calvary reminded us of the great love of Christ for all of us. In some ways it concentrated on the personal, one-to-one, relationship between myself and Jesus. Jesus loved me so much that he died for me. I came to Mass to praise and thank him. The presence of Jesus in the Blessed Sacrament gave me further opportunity for a solid, person-to-person relationship with him.

Another way of viewing the Mass was to see it as celebration. We have experienced a great deal of this idea in modern times. We come together to celebrate the fact that we are so loved by God that he remains with us in the Eucharistic presence. We create a sort of 'party mood' at Mass so that we might be more aware of the marvel of such a love. We celebrate being chosen as his people. We celebrate his presence in our world. We celebrate the wonders of life and creation that he has given us. When we gather at Mass, we give to the Father worship and praise and thanksgiving together with Jesus who is present to us. No longer do I concentrate simply on my own person-to-person relationship with the Lord, but expand it to realize that we, as a people, worship our Father. We are his people; he is our God, and we gather together at Mass to celebrate the wonder of that relationship.

We might also see the Mass as a special meal or banquet. In this concept we reflect the elements of the Last Supper where our Lord sat at table with his friends and broke bread with them. There is the beautiful sign of friendship here, for those who sit at table with one another must live and act as friends. Here we are one with Jesus and each other. When we have eaten with a brother, we ought not to raise our hand or voice against him. At the table of the Lord we are nourished and strengthened for the work of the Lord. Most especially, at the table of the Lord there must be reconciliation and peace. We are friends. Friends to Jesus and friends to each other. This contact with Jesus requires living out the commitment of friendship wherever we may be. It moves us to deeper communal love.

Each of these explanations adds something to our understanding of the Eucharist. The reality of the Eucharist embraces all three, just as any one of the three in isolation can lead to half-faithful lives. Should we stress the "meal" aspect and the need for an extroverted spirituality, we might succumb to the rat-race mentality that puts action in conflict with prayer and reflection. The self-centered spirituality that can grow from the over-stress of the "sacrifice" explanation can overdo attention to oneself to the loss of real charity that must expand to embrace others. Sometimes, the "celebration" can be so noisy that there is no room to listen in reflective quiet for the word of the Lord.

It seems to me that at different times we shall be in need of each element of Eucharist. Sometimes I need a quiet, one-to-one relationship with the Eucharistic Jesus. I need to be aware, personally, of how important it is to be one with him. I may not remain in my own little cocoon, but I may need to spend some time there to strengthen my personal relationship with God and his Son, Jesus. At other times I may sense the need to celebrate God's goodness to me. A goodness that I could never express alone. So I join with fellow believers to praise our Lord with one harmonious voice of song and praise, a celebration of joy in the presence of Jesus. But often I need to be reminded of the responsibility that 'breaking bread' together requires of me. I can't be satisfied with bumper sticker slogans about loving one another. When I gather at the table of the Lord, joining in sharing a meal with my brothers and sisters and Jesus, I am

called to the hard consequences of being 'one.' The need to
forgive another so that we can live our oneness is not always
easy. The need to support another and avoid petty gossip
and tearing down with word and action is not easy. But the
sign of being at table together asks this of us. The Eucharist
is a place that calls for total and absolute dedication
to Jesus. It is an impossible dream made possible through
the presence of Jesus.

As Franciscans we shall find that our fraternity life shall
require us to be a people who live out the commitment that
the Eucharist calls us to. There is no smallness about the call
of Jesus. Again and again, at every Eucharistic celebration,
he calls us to do as he does, to give ourselves completely to
him as he gives himself completely to us. Very early in
his life as a Trappist, Thomas Merton wrote these words
about the Mass. They apply to all of us, not simply to
priests.

> The Mass has made an end forever of what I used to
> treasure as an interior solitude. It has shown me the way
> to a height of solitude I never dreamed of because its
> paradox was utterly beyond my own imagining. This is
> the solitude of Christ in the Blessed Sacrament. Jesus
> in the host is alone, not because he is remote and
> isolated from everybody, but because he is given to
> everybody, given utterly! And because he is given to
> everybody, he can belong exclusively to nobody. And
> yet he is so alone that he belongs entirely to each one
> who possesses him.

> If you are afraid of love, never become a priest, never
> say Mass. The Mass will draw down upon your soul a
> torrent of interior suffering which has only one function
> —to break you wide open and let everybody in the
> world into your heart. If you are afraid of people, never
> say Mass! If you want to guard against invasion, never

say Mass! For when you begin to say Mass, the Spirit of God awakes like a giant inside you and bursts the lock of your private sanctuary and calls all the people in the world to come into your heart. If you say Mass, you condemn your soul to a torment of a love that is so vast and so insatiable that you will never be able to bear it alone. That love is the love of the heart of Jesus, burning within your own miserable heart, and bringing down upon you the huge weight of his pity for all the sins of the world.

Do you know what that love will do to you if you let it work in your soul? If you do not resist it? It will devour you! It will kill you! It will break your heart!

. . . Without actually doing violence to your heart (for Christ's love always works with a power that is smooth and delicate, even when it smashes you) the Spirit strikes like lightning as soon as there is the slightest opening in your will and in a flash he is upon you with his new demand. And almost every time it seems to be a sweeping demand for your whole self, everything, a holocaust!

Where is there a hiding place, where is there a mountain or an unvisited desert where a poor priest can go to escape the voices of men that are brought to the ears of his soul by the Holy Spirit? Where can a creature without courage and without virtue, and almost without faith, hide his head and blot out the image of the faces that look at him and the hands that reach out to him? Where can he go to stop his ears against the voices that cry: "Die for me! Die for me!"

That is not all. It is not only the ones we must die for that terrify us, it is most of all the ones we must live for. They demand not only our strength and our health and our time, but if we listen to the voice of Christ in them, there will be many who claim, as an imperious right, the deepest recesses of your heart and soul, because we are their Christ and we have to love them with the same love with which Christ loves them ... It is not enough to be a mere agent of God, transacting his business and then retiring within ourselves. We have to do the work of him who sent us, which is to live consumed in the suffering of love.

Where I found Christ, Edited by John O'Brien

This is what we are called to live when we celebrate the sacrifice of the Mass. It is a call to the deepest kind of poverty; a call to empty oneself so that the Spirit may move freely in our lives. It contains within itself both the challenge of the gospel and the companion who can help us live the gospel. We know that this poverty does not just happen. Our Eucharistic participation will depend on our daily relationships with Jesus. The way in which our lives are lived will color the way we celebrate. The constancy of our prayer-relationship with Jesus day by day will determine the intensity of our prayer together at Eucharist. Our growing concern for the brethren will find its impetus here. Our ability to walk together shall come from our unity around this table of the Lord. At the heart of the Franciscan life is Christ. Eucharist brings us together with him so that we might walk together with him as we share with the brethren. His riches, his presence is shared with us even to dying. He looks for the same dedication from us and then communes with us to make it possible. Give praise to this Lord and brother of ours who comes to us in Eucharist, simply and completely. Respond in like manner.

14. Love Is for Real People

THERE IS DELIGHT IN SEEING THE JOY OF A child who is loved. There is a sense of awe in viewing the sweeping majesty of a valley from a mountain top. There is a moment of quiet acceptance when two people in love are with one another. Love brings joy. Love also pays the price to get to joy.

The two great commandments of Jesus ask for wholehearted love. The love Jesus asks for is not simply a sentimental, romantic thing based on emotion. Real love requires much more than the feelings of love. Jesus knew real love and it brought him to Gethsemane and Calvary and resurrection. Real love will follow the pattern of dying and rising; suffering and joy. It is the pattern we see in the life of Christ. It is the pattern we see in Francis. It will be our pattern as well.

I find myself returning often to the slopes of Calvary and to the rocky soil of Gethsemane to gain strength for living. There I see Jesus suffer the agony of making his personal decision in favor of his Father's will. His struggle is my struggle or vice versa if you prefer. But the Father meant everything to Jesus. Their intimate relationship could not be fractured even in the face of death. To do the Father's will may not be what I want at any given moment. Faith tells me then that love is still at work even when the Father seems quiet in the face of my need.

It would be sheer foolishness to talk about the Franciscan way of life without talking about the passion, death and resurrection of Jesus. I cannot substitute emotional ecstacy for persistent love. I cannot speak of the 'good news' and refuse to stand beneath a cross as I proclaim it. I will come to joy and to life, for that is what Jesus promised. But my emptying out, my dying, my yielding to the Lord will take me to Calvary before I reach the Sunday morning in the garden of resurrection. I shall live this pattern again and again. It will be the way to Jesus and through him to the Father. The Spirit shall push and prod and inspire me so that I know the truth and give witness to it.

> I solemnly assure you, unless the grain of wheat falls to the earth and dies, it remains just a grain of wheat. But if it dies, it produces much fruit. The man who loves his life, loses it, while the man who hates his life in this world preserves it to life eternal. If anyone would serve me, let him follow me; where I am, there will my servant be.
>
> John 12: 24 - 26

Always the call is to life. Always the way to life is through letting loose of one's own life for the sake of Jesus. This touches on the absolute poverty we are called to embrace, to yield ourselves, to hand ourselves over to the Lord. The promised result is life and joy and peace and gentleness and the other gifts the Spirit brings.

St Paul often spoke of the resurrection in his early preaching. It did not seem to draw people by itself. He was received politely, but nothing happened in the lives of the people who heard him. Little by little Paul changed the tenor of his preaching. He began to speak about the passion, cross *and* resurrection of Jesus. He found that the power of this word of God did what he was unable to do, it helped men accept their need for Jesus and conversion.

For Christ did not send me to baptize, but to preach the

gospel—not with wordy 'wisdom,' however, lest the cross of Christ be rendered void of its meaning. The message of the cross is complete absurdity to those who are headed for ruin, but to us who are experiencing salvation it is the power of God. Scripture says; "I will destroy the wisdom of the wise, and thwart the cleverness of the clever." Where is the wise man to be found? Where the scribe? Where is the master of worldly argument? Has not God turned the wisdom of this world into folly? Since in God's wisdom the world did not come to know him through 'wisdom'; it pleased God to save those who believe through the absurdity of the preaching of the gospel. Yes, the Jews demand 'signs' and Greeks look for 'wisdom,' but we preach Christ crucified—a stumbling block to Jews, and an absurdity to Gentiles; but to those who are called, Jews and Greeks alike, Christ, the power of God and the wisdom of God. For God's folly is wiser than men, and his weakness more powerful than men.

1 Corinthians 1: 17 - 25

Paul's strong words about the cross clearly reveal it as a powerful and essential force in the Christian life. This cross is a sign of love and life. It is a finger pointing to God and stretching our spirit so that we might become all that we can be. It is the sign that Francis received in his stigmata, etching its marks on his body. It was in a moment before the crucifix of San Damiano that he began his journey to the dream of the gospel. To follow Francis is to accept the sacrifice of one's life for the sake of the Lord. To follow Francis is to accept self-sacrifice and discipline for the sake of the gospel.

In our own time there is a special need for this kind of witness to the cross. Too often we are willing to settle for a 'comfortable' gospel, an easy way of life in coming to the Father. We would do mountainous damage to people were our love only a seeking for self-fulfillment. It is a sad 'joke' that in our time the search for personal fulfillment has discarded the way of the cross as the way to life. While suffering exists all around us and within us, we run away from it. Loneliness, fear, boredom, isolation and impersonalism all reveal themselves in the eyes of many people of our time. We seek pleasure with a passion and come away empty hearted. We use artificial stimulants to achieve joy, and the moment turns to ashes that compounds our sadness. In our passion for progress, we have become the slaves of a million masters. Francis of Assisi did not philosophize about all of this. He simply and directly showed men the way to joy. It is the way of Jesus and his gospel and it includes the cross. Even when we seek the Lord we can still mis-interpret the message.

> It is possible to be so eager to do something for God and for souls as to forget that what God needs for new witness to his love is not people who can do something, but people through whom He can do something.
>
> *Marginals*, Sister Mary Francis, 45

God's way of doing things is found in the pattern of the life of his Son, Jesus Christ. It is the Word-made-flesh who stands as the model and example for our lives. This is how Francis says it and it must become our way as well. To Jesus, the will of his Father was a vital part of being Jesus. In his first words to a puzzled Mary and Joseph in the temple, he asks a simple direct question:

"Did you not know I must be about my Father's business?" Though Mary was puzzled, Jesus already is clear in showing how vital the Father's will is to him. Again and again throughout his preaching, he refers to the importance of doing the Father's will. Even in the last moments of life, after an agony in the Garden that wrung blood from his body, he still must accept that will of the Father. On the cross, though the Father seems to have abandoned him, he still finally cries out: "Into your hands, Father, I commend my spirit." There is an identification with the Father that means everything to Jesus. It is an influence that is in the forefront of his awareness. It is such a model that Francis tried to imitate. From the moment of naked aloneness in the court of the Bishop, Francis stood ready to accept the Father as his father. This same heavenly Father sent his only Son to teach us the truth and show us the way. For Francis there was nothing else possible except to accept the gospel and all its implications. His life begins to be a more and more perfect reflection of the gospel truth. Francis serves as an example of how the gospel is to be lived and that it is possible to live it. Francis does not hinder our following of Jesus or stand between ourselves and Jesus. Quite the contrary. His faith in Jesus urges us on to go and do likewise. His joy is clear indication that the promises of Christ are realized and not just pipe dreams. Francis of Assisi is unique and special. His absolute acceptance of the gospel gives him a special place in the history of salvation.

. . . Francis of Assisi shows an evangelical note, an immediacy to the gospel, which has also carried over to his order in a way not characteristic of the others. Perhaps we can simply say: *Francis wanted nothing else but to live the gospel* . . . What he actually wants is the gospel and nothing but the gospel.

In general, Francis did not have a problem with the question: What does the gospel *mean*? Thus he was more taken up with another question: Why was the gospel no longer operative and effective? People did not *live* according to the gospel! . . . And the way to combat the situation was just as direct and simple: somebody must begin to do that again. Simply, straightforwardly, without sophistry, without adding or subtracting anything, someone had to *live the gospel* and nothing else!

Living our Future, von Galli, 54 & 66

Doing that precise thing is what we are called to do in our own time as we follow the Franciscan way of life. Francis spoke so clearly about the gospel:

> I am the servant of all and so I am bound to wait upon everyone and make known to them the fragrant words of my Lord. Realizing, however, that because of my sickness and ill-health, I cannot personally visit each one individually, I decided to send you a letter bringing a message with the words of our Lord Jesus Christ, who is the Word of the Father, and of the Holy Spirit, whose words are spirit and life. (John 6:64)

> Our Lord Jesus Christ is the glorious word of the Father, so holy and exalted, whose coming the Father made known by St Gabriel the archangel to the glorious and blessed virgin Mary, in whose womb he took on our weak human nature. He was rich beyond measure and yet he and his holy mother chose poverty.
>
> *Writings of St Francis*, Fahey-Hermann, 93

How important to Francis are the 'words of our Lord Jesus Christ.' How he longed to share them with his brethren. How he recognized the poverty of Jesus, the 'handing over' that Jesus embraced in doing the will of his Father.

Real love shall be built on such a poverty and such a handing over to the Lord. As we grow aware of our personal poverty we shall be able to be filled up with Christ. It is not a false, "I'm a no-good person" that we speak about here. Rather, it is the recognition of a littleness that needs a savior in order to learn how to love. It is a faith in Jesus that knows how great is his love and how he wishes us to be his channels for love. This lavish sharing by Jesus, his own love coming to us and becoming our own, enriches our ability to love others. But it requires us to die so that the Lord may live in us, totally and completely. It is the cycle of dying and rising that shall fill our life until we pass over to the Lord through the doorway of death. I shall enrich my neighbor not simply by sharing my own, limited human abilities and love, but through the generous sharing of the love poured into my heart by my loving savior. Such a sharing requires open hands and open hearts that are ready to be emptied out in order to be filled with the Lord and the power of his Spirit. In short, our ability to love in this life shall be closely linked to the measure of our faith. Great as is the praise St Paul lavishes on love or charity in his letter to the Corinthians, it is linked closely with faith and hope, until they are no longer needed and love alone remains.

If we are going to understand the love of Jesus we need to go to Jesus. Sensitivity sessions, using the findings of psychology and behavorial scientists can be a help along the way. But they cannot supply for faith. They may help our inter-personal relationships, but they will not be enough to fulfill the two great commandments of the Lord in the manner he calls for.

> We are presently somewhat preoccupied with personal-ity and the development of natural gifts. It might be better merely to be occupied. For it is good and proper to insist that grace builds on nature, but it is important that we clarify what it is in nature that grace builds on. We have the holy paradox . . . that we must develop each his own nature and yet be at enmity with nature. The key to the paradox lies in the very simplest of expressions: a supernatural life. It is to this that we are called, to a life not stifling or destroying nature, but definitely above nature.
>
> *Marginals*, Sister Mary Francis, 44

Activity will never be able to substitute for knowing Jesus. All the inter-personal skills will not make me a good follower of Jesus if it remains on a merely human level of love. Looking to 'find Jesus in people' will never happen if I know nothing of Jesus and do not know who I am looking for. I will need to know Jesus directly through faith. I will need to pray. Christ's identification with his poor and his people were not meant as a substitute for knowing him as he is in himself. The faith-knowledge shall lead to love that reflects the love of Jesus. It would be a half-truth or less to follow a religion of 'finding Christ only in people.' This is not the way of Francis. Should others be able to accomplish such a task, more power to them. For us the way is through Jesus. Otherwise ours shall become a "Gee, I feel good" kind of religion that may be a simple masquerade for self-love.

> To say everything one thinks, to do everything one likes, to decide all things for oneself, is to bring forth green leaves likely enough—like poison ivy!
>
> *Marginals*, Sister Mary Francis, 45

Both Jesus and Mary give us solid examples of the willingness of lovers whose faith dominates their decisions. Both were dominated by the will of the Father. For Mary it was often a mystery to be pondered. For Jesus it was a thirst to be quenched at the living waters of the Father's love for him. For both of them it led to a cross where they suffered, lovingly, together because of their commitment to the Father. The manner in which Jesus loved others also shows the results of the Father's influence. His love expressed itself in the way that was needed at any particular moment. To Peter he was strong: "Get behind me, Satan. You think like a man and not like God." Yet on another occasion he could pull a wet Peter from the water and simply chide him with a "O, you of little faith!" His love for the Pharisees showed itself in a clearcut condemnation of some of their hypocrisy, yet he was courteous to Nicodemus when he came to see Jesus at night. Gentleness marked his dealings with the women who wiped his feet while he dined in Simon's house. Sorrow filled his heart as he asked Judas to do quickly what he had to do. Compassion for the crowds was his love's expression for the people who seemed like sheep without a shepherd. On the cross, his concern was to forgive the men who nailed him to the cross.

Even a brief survey of the "how" of Christ's love puts it at a point quite different from some of the modern gush about love. The way of Jesus brings us to wholeness and integrity. It may not be easy, but it is the way he leads. When we are whole, we are good channels of the love of Jesus, allowing it to flow through us to others. The price of such a life is death. The man who seeks to save his life, to have everything his own way, will lose his life and perhaps also lose his way.

> I solemnly assure you, unless the grain of wheat falls to the earth and dies, it remains just a grain of wheat. But if it dies, it produces much fruit. The man who loves his life, loses it, while the man who hates his life in this world preserves it to life eternal.
>
> John 12: 24 - 25

To walk this path, to travel this way, will require of us a yielding to the Lord, handing ourselves in trust to the Lord. Again the Lord makes it clear that this trust must be given him if we would hope to deepen our love-life.

> Whoever puts faith in me believes not so much in me as in him who sent me; and whoever looks on me is seeing him who sent me. I have come to the world as its light, to keep anyone who believes in me from remaining in the dark. If anyone hears my words and does not keep them, I am not the one to condemn him, for I

did not come to condemn the world but to save it. Whoever rejects me and does not accept my words already has his judge, namely, the word I have spoken—it is that which will condemn him on the last day. For I have not spoken on my own; no, the Father who sent me has commanded me what to say and how to speak. Since I know that his commandment means eternal life, whatever I say is spoken just as he instructed me.

John 12: 44 - 50

The result of both hearing the word of the Lord and living it in practice is life, both now and after death. Always we can move ahead confidently because Jesus is with us. We never are alone in this seeking for being perfect as the Father is perfect. The assurance of Jesus gives us courage:

'Peace' is my farewell to you, my peace is my gift to you; I do not give it to you as the world gives peace. Do not be distressed or fearful. You have heard me say, "I go away for a while, and I come back to you." If you truly loved me you would rejoice to have me go to the Father, for the Father is greater than I. I tell you this now, before it takes place, so that when it takes place you may believe. I shall not go on speaking to you longer; the Prince of this world is at hand. He has no hold on me but the world must know that I love the Father and do as the Father has commanded me. Come, then! Let us be on our way.

John 14: 27 - 31

As the Father has loved me, so I have loved you. Live on in my love. You will live in my love if you keep my commandments, even as I have kept my Father's commandments, and live in his love. All this I tell you that my joy may be yours and your joy may be complete . . . I no longer speak of you as slaves, for a

slave does not know what his master is about. Instead
I call you friends, since I have made known to you all
that I heard from my Father.

John 15: 9 - 15

I have given them the glory you gave me that they may
be one, as we are one—I living in them, you living in
me—that their unity may be complete. So shall the
world know that you sent me, and that you loved them
as you loved me. Father, all those you gave me I would
have in my company where I am, to see this glory of
mine which is your gift to me, because of the love you
bore me before the world began. Just Father, the world
has not known you, but I have known you; and
these men have known that you sent me. To them I have
revealed your name, and I will continue to reveal it so
that your love for me may live in them, and I may live
in them.

John 17: 22 - 26

Jesus lives in us! There is the heart of our strength and
courage to follow his gospel. The prayer of Jesus is always
answered by the Father. His prayer for our joy, his prayer to
live with us is certain to be answered. Jesus is the foundation
of our ability to love one another as he has loved us. Without
Him we could not do that. His compassion for us, his coming
to us is the one thing that makes real love possible. It
enlarges our hearts and stretches our spirit so that the love of
Christ may enter our heart and the Spirit of Jesus activate
our own spirit. Thus shall we be ready to love as Jesus has
loved us. Francis knew his need for Jesus and knew his own
poverty. Thus he sought Jesus and became deeply aware that
God is everything, "My God and my all!"

A sound tradition of realistic, identifying love belongs
to Franciscans. A son or daughter of Francis is never so

estranged from the spirit of the founder as when he does not love in this identifying manner. St Francis always wanted to experience the pain of others, the beggar, the leper, and—in his prayer on Mount Alverna—the redeeming Christ. He always wanted to see things just as they were . . . The Church of the 13th century needed to purify itself of triumphalism, of riches, of splendid trappings. So, instead of attacking the Church, Francis was himself poor. Lepers were despised and avoided. So, instead of belaboring society, Francis himself sought them out and washed and cared for them. And so with other conditions, with other needs. It was a terribly realistic approach he had. To return to the "original spirit of his institute," to his "spirit and special aims," demands that we *become* as little children. Because we are not.

Marginals, Sister Mary Francis, 21

To trust as a child trusts is what Jesus asks. Our society often counters that plea with a cry for "Independence!" "Liberation" and similar cries for so-called freedom. Yet the cries have not brought us peace. So faith brings us back to the gospel and the need to trust the one whom we love, namely, Jesus. It does take a single-minded person to accept not only the will of the Father but also the consequences of accepting the will of the Father. It will require an intense searching for the will of the Father when the issues and/or events may cover his will in an apparent fog of confusion and doubt. To continue to love Jesus and to seek the Father shall require the power of the Holy Spirit. But it shall require more than human feelings of love. Rather, it shall be ready to give the whole of life to the direction of the Spirit of Jesus. Such a love will require a deep faith in Jesus.

Such a love will show itself in the whole of life. It will influence and color our attitudes to people, events, and creation; it will touch the perspective with which we judge things and people in our lives; it will move us to take time for prayer and for people; it will lead us, like John the Baptist, to say: "He must increase and I must decrease." In the final chapter of this love, it will bring us to the point where we can say with St Paul: "It is no longer I who live, but Christ lives in me." All of this will be done wherever we may be. Whether we are married or single, priest or brother, widow or widower, sick or well, this shall be the way we shall learn to love with all our heart and soul and mind and strength. For when we love God in this way, we shall be sent by our Father to share that love with our neighbor.

If a life without love is a nothing, then following Francis without stretching your ability to love falls into the same category. It cannot be repeated too often that the price of love is the total gift of oneself. It is *not* simply in sex or pleasure; it is *not* in material gifts showered on the loved one. It is *not* even giving food and drink to those in need. These are the expressions of a love that must live in one's heart. But if the heart is empty, the actions cannot substitute for the real thing. Our cycle of coming to God is full of this process of learning to love. From an inner growth in love to the actions of love and then the reflective opening to Jesus and then the whole process repeated again and again in our lives. In the life of Francis, as in our own, the way to love and wisdom is the way of Jesus. Francis' seeking of love, however spontaneous it was, did not escape the universal law of trial and error, of constantly learning better ways to express love. The love in the heart of Francis matured slowly as he faced the reality of the demands of Jesus. It was not easy for Francis, but he accepted, in fact, embraced, the way of the gospel even when it was not clear. He readily realized that he did not yet know fully the will of God for tomorrow, so he responded to the best of his ability as he understood it for today. Such response brought him to his tomorrows ready to sense and do the will of the Father. Even in his agony over the strife and dissension in his Order he was able to draw closer to the Lord. He looked not only to the failure he experienced, but to the seed of hope the Lord planted in the middle of the field of failure.

> This crisis (in the Order) was a terrible trial for Francis. He felt himself a failure. But God was there waiting for him: it was a supreme purification. With a shattered spirit, the Poor One of Assisi proceeded toward a complete and definitive renunciation of himself. Through misery and tears, he was at last to attain peace and joy. At the same time, he saved his own friars by disclosing to them that the most exalted form of evangelical poverty is also the most realistic: it is one in which man acknowledges and accepts reality, both human and divine, reality in all its dimensions. It was the way to salvation for his Order; a way which did not isolate itself in a sort of protestantism before Luther, but found within the Church herself an interior equilibrium and permanence.
>
> *Wisdom of the Poverello*, Leclerc, xlv

Our own pattern for learning to love or learning the 'how' of love will reflect the pattern of Jesus and Francis. We shall not escape the road of suffering and purification. It will also bring us to moments of quiet exaltation. But underlying all of it shall be the firm confidence that the Father loves us. The confidence that his creative love can lead us to whatever heights he wants us to climb. Jesus passed through the glory of Mt Tabor and endured the agony of Gethsemane and Calvary because the Father's love was his. Even when the Father seems to have abandoned us, he is still present and looking forward to our moment of life and joy. Suffering and purification find meaning in resurrection. But resurrection finds meaning and value in suffering and purification. It is one whole garment. The reality of true love finds expression in the words of St Paul even while these same words serve as a strong challenge to our love and our need to grow in love.

Your love must be sincere. Detest what is evil, cling to what is good. Love one another with the affection of brothers. Anticipate each other in showing respect. Do not grow slack but be fervent in spirit; he whom you serve is the Lord. Rejoice in hope, be patient under trial, persevere in prayer. Look on the needs of the saints as your own; be generous in offering hospitality. Bless your persecutors; bless and do not curse them. Rejoice with those who rejoice, weep with those who weep. Have the same attitude toward all. Put away ambitious thoughts and associate with those who are lowly. Do not be wise in your own estimation. Never repay injury with injury. See that your conduct is honorable in the eyes of all. If possible, live peaceably with everyone.

Romans 12: 9 - 18

In the name of the encouragement you owe me in Christ, in the name of the solace that love can give, of fellowship in spirit, compassion, and pity, I beg you: make my joy complete by your unanimity, possessing the one love, united in spirit and ideals. Never act out of rivalry and conceit: rather, let all parties think humbly of others as superior to themselves, each of you looking to others' interests rather than to his own.

Your attitude must be that of Christ: though he was in the form of God, he did not deem equality with God something to be grasped at. Rather he emptied himself and took the form of a slave, being born in the likeness of men. He was known to be of human estate and it was thus that he humbled himself obediently accepting even death, death on a cross. Because of this, God highly exalted him and bestowed on him the name above every other name, so that at Jesus' name every knee must bend in the heavens, on the earth, and under the earth, and every tongue proclaim to the glory of God the Father: JESUS CHRIST IS LORD!

Philippians 2: 1 - 11

Our honest and sincere acceptance of the reality of true love and all of its consequences will bring us once more to the Lord. We will need him to fulfill such a love. With faith in our Father, walking with the Lord and open to the Spirit, we shall be able to accomplish the goal of real love — unity with Jesus and through him to the Father under the inspiration of the Spirit who shall move us to unity with each other. Then Jesus' prayer will be accomplished in us: "By this will all men know you are my disciples, if you have love, one for another."

15. Listen to the Word of the Lord

THE GOSPEL IS OUR WAY OF LIFE. It is the Word-made-flesh speaking to us through his written word. As our way to the Father it is of vital and fundamental importance in our lives.

The Bible is a book of a living word. Most other books are finished when they are written; beginning, middle and end, and that's it. It is a product produced. The Bible still speaks in this time and in this place as though no time had passed. The same message of Jesus is being given to us through the Bible. It is not a book for 'back there' or for a people who lived at 'another time.' As a living word of the Lord it is meant for here and it is meant for now—for the here and now of the lives of each one of us. It is a word of faith and requires faith so that we hear it rightly. God continues to speak to us and his wisdom is still available to us in this age. We are not second-class citizens of the Kingdom, having to be satisfied with second hand writings. The Bible is as much for my time and my life as it was for Magdelene or Lazarus who saw the Lord visibly and heard his words with their own ears. There is a timelessness to this word, but also a very direct communication from the Lord.

To be able to hear the word of the Lord in the Scriptures, we will need to possess some qualities of faith. Poverty, faithfulness, joy are among the requirements for the hearing of the word. We don't expect that everyone can be a Scripture scholar, able to know the details of history and culture of biblical times. But if this word of Jesus is going to take root in us, the soil of our lives will need preparation so that the seed of the word may fall on fertile ground.

> Just as the life of the Church is strengthened through the frequent celebration of the Eucharistic mystery, similarly we may hope for a new stimulus for the life of the Spirit from a growing reverence for the Word of God which lasts forever. (Is 40: 8 - 1 Peter 1: 23 - 25)
> *Constitution on Divine Revelation*, #26

As followers of Francis of Assisi we are specially called to be a people to whom the gospel is second nature. Francis himself put it this way:

> It is good to read what the Scripture testifies, good to seek out our Lord in it. For my part, I have fixed in mind so much of the Scriptures that it now suffices most amply for my meditation and reflection. I do not need very much, my son; I know about poor Christ crucified.
> *Words of St Francis*, #151

If we wish to allow the living word of the Bible into our lives we must be ready to accept that word. If we do, it will begin to change our way of looking at things; it will affect our attitude toward people and problems; it will touch our judgements about people and the values that govern our lives; it will lead us to compassion and gentleness as well as forgiveness and understanding. The Bible will speak to our heart about the need for conversion and further generosity. It will call us to prayer and a more intense response to the will of the Father. If we allow it to do so, it shall take possession of us and make us one with Jesus.

All of this requires faith. It is the root disposition for hearing the word of the Lord in Scripture. We need to believe in God and his Son and in the power of his Spirit. It requires the identification with Jesus in faith that makes him the center of our life and growth. As we move to grow in the faith, his word in Scripture becomes more and more important. We hear the words differently because we are better attuned to listen in faith. Throughout our lives we shall find new insight into the meaning of the word of the Lord. It is Jesus' way of leading us to a deeper intimacy with himself. Without faith in Jesus, the Scriptures are simply nice words and perhaps inspiring thoughts. Faith makes those words a driving force in our lives that turns everything else upside down.

> Faith is an attitude, a profound and flexible driving force which directs without bludgeoning, enlightens without dazzling, and judges without prejudicing. Its aim is to educe and foster the potentialities of the human mind, not to supplant them.

> . . . (The man of faith) learns to bow to the grandeur of the mysteries of God and to admit his own inadequacy. His horizon is widened, and he becomes a realist. He learns prudence because he learns to know his own weakness. He becomes at the same time bold and daring, because he is not afraid of being found in the wrong. Rather than manipulate the smallest detail of a truth of faith or reason, he will suspend judgement. Faith is the best school for learning clear-sightedness and common sense. Along with simple and bold humility, common sense is perhaps faith's most indispensable contribution to the understanding of the Bible. Common sense is the right appreciation of reality, and nothing is more real than faith. It preserves man from the scruples of the faint-hearted and the extravagances of the rationalist.
> *Christian approach to the Bible*, Charlier, 249f

Only the man who has the openness of faith can hear the

clear voice of the Lord in the Scriptures. His common sense sees that reality is linked to God and without God reality is a sham and a mockery. By the same token, the man of faith accepts the consequences of his belief no matter what the cost. He grows steadily in this acceptance, but this is the path that he follows until the Lord is everything for him.

Poverty or abandonment is another quality we ought to bring to the hearing of the word. It is all too easy to come to the Bible with some pre-conceived notions or ideas or opinions. We look in the Scriptures to find conclusive evidence for conclusions we have already reached. So we read the word with a biased mind and the Spirit finds it hard to break through this crust of bias or pre-conceptions. We can find ourselves looking for texts to support some action we want to take—and we will probably find something that seems to fit. We look to Scripture to prove our side of an argument—and it will probably be there in some form. It is one means we use to force Scripture to say to us what we want to hear. If we are poor such a process is unthinkable. We come to this word of God knowing our littleness and our need for the Lord. We come without our hands and hearts full of what we want to hear. We come open-handed and open-hearted to listen to what the Lord is saying. We put aside our fears of hearing things that are too disturbing and stand ready for whatever he wishes to say to us. This kind of abandonment is not easy, for our minds are often cluttered with things that stand in the way of open listening. Yet we will sooner or later catch a glimpse of the power of this word if we continue to seek to be poor and to abandon ourselves to the Lord. Francis of Assisi approached the Bible as a poor man. He handed himself over to the word, allowing its words to sink into his spirit and take root there and make its demand there and bring its joys there. Each time he came, there was a difference in him that allowed for a sharper insight or a greater abandonment to this word. He wished to accept it simply, plainly and without glossing it over to suit his fancy. He took it seriously and recognized that here was a living word spoken by his Lord and Brother, Jesus Christ, and by the Spirit that Jesus had sent.

The quality of joy is needed because the Scriptures, even when they ask us to carry the cross, mean to lead us to life and joy. Perhaps joy is not only a quality for coming to the Bible but also a quality the Bible gives to us. True joy refreshes and sensitizes the spirit. We become more aware of life and love. Such a quality has obvious advantages in coming to the written word of the Lord. Joy creates a readiness to listen and a sensitiveness to understand. It clears away fears and frustrations so that the Spirit can reach into our lives without obstacles blocking the way. Like the little children who so readily accept what they hear from people they love, so we accept joyfully the word from our Beloved and let it sink into our hearts.

The Bible carries us along on its passage through history. It shows us a people chosen by God simply because He so decided. It was not their greatness that accomplished the call, but God's choice of them no matter what their condition or worth. Thus does God reveal himself in Scripture as the initiator of loving and saving actions to his people. Even when they are unfaithful, he still reaches out to them in love.

This same consistent love reaches out for us today. The gospel reveals the loving God taking flesh, "putting on skin" for our sakes. The Son becomes like us in all things but sin. His gospel message calls us to unity with the Father through Jesus. It spells out the way to the Kingdom through a man-God who is the way. His way of life, his truth, is the rock on which we build our lives.

The Bible calls us to a total giving to our Father, Francis, in his almost reckless abandonment to God, puts us in touch with reality. Until we too come to such a radical handing over of life to the Lord, we try to tame and contain God. He constantly eludes our grasp and moves beyond the limitations we would impose on him. Handing ourselves over to God is putting ourselves at the disposal of a whirlwind or an earthquake, or, at times, a gentle breeze. But always the call goes out for everything within us to be His. The gospel shall continue to reveal the extent of that call and the power of the dream of Jesus.

Franciscans will necessarily become a people who absorb the words of the gospel and make them their very own. It is helpful to know the history, the culture, the perspective of the people who wrote the Bible. It can help in understanding the Bible. But it is not absolutely essential —only helpful. It seems to me that anyone, no matter what their level of educational achievement, can come to the gospel and be taught. Coming to the Scriptures with an open faith and honesty, with a poorness that is ready to be filled, will make us the recipients of the message of the gospel, for the poor will understand the words addressed to them by Jesus. There is a gentle wisdom, for example, in not trying to read the Bible from cover to cover as a sort of disciplined exercise. There is no harm in it, but it may lose some of its power if it simply becomes an endurance contest. But moving from familiar New Testament readings with a gradual turning to the Old Testament to understand the new, will be a more effective way of listening to the word. Moving quietly to understand things like Passover and the Old Law will lead from New Testament words to an exploration of their meaning in the Old Testament. Then the words of Jonah or of Jeremiah may become gradually familiar. Thus the Word leads us to deeper knowledge and acceptance as the Bible comes more alive for us. For, finally, this word is meant to help us change our lives and not simply fill our minds. The man of faith shall be able to understand this and continue to seek out the Word for his life. The Bible shall be vitally important in such a search. For a follower of Francis, it shall always be a number one way of knowing Jesus.

Mary, a model of faith

Mary is one who gives us a model of the kind of faith that
we need in coming to her son. The gospels describe her as a
woman who often had to ponder God's ways in her heart.
She was a reflective person, for she gave an acceptance to the
Father's will even when she did not understand the 'why' of
it. But she did not draw back from her commitment to be
the 'handmaid of the Lord.' She really meant it when she
said: "Be it done to me according to your word."

Small wonder, then, that Francis was devoted to Mary.
Throughout his life he maintained a deep and tender devotion to her. It was in the little Church of Mary of the Angels
that he often prayed. Her faith strengthened his faith. He
praised her in these beautiful words:

> Hail, Holy Lady, most holy Queen
> Mary, Mother of God, ever virgin
> Chosen by the most holy Father in heaven
> Consecrated by him, with his most beloved son and
> the Holy Spirit, the comforter.
> On you descended and in you still remains all the
> fullness of grace and every good.
> Hail, his palace. Hail, his tabernacle.
> Hail, his robe. Hail, his handmaid.
> Hail, his mother.
> *Writings of St Francis*, Fahey-Hermann, 135 - 136

Thomas of Celano, the first biographer of St Francis says
that Francis was filled with an inexpressible love of Mary
because it was "she who made the Lord of majesty our
brother." Francis recognized a kindred spirit in Mary as one
who believed strongly and responded fully to the Father.
Though he had his own personal devotion to our Lady, he
recognized that it was not prayers or devotions alone that
bring her honor. They are only part of the story. Someone

who really is dedicated to Mary shall become, like her, a person of faith. Not only shall prayers be offered to this Mother, but life shall express the fact that we understand her call to BE like Jesus, her son. Mary is not a substitute for Jesus. She is his mother. Because God has given her a special place in his plan of salvation, we too shall give her special honor. Most especially, our lives shall reflect hers as we faithfully listen to the message of Jesus. Here again, Francis shows his sense of faith by maintaining the delicate balance of devotion to Mary without making it everything in life. As with the saints and other holy men and women, Mary leads us to her son. Her rosary, her apparitions, particular devotions to her are indeed good and worthwhile. But the criterion of their value in our life is the manner in which they bring us to Jesus and to his gospel. Mary is not our savior.

> There is but one mediator as we know from the words of the Apostle: "For there is one God and one mediator of God and men, the man Jesus Christ, who gave himself as redemption for all." (1 Tim 2: 5-6) The maternal duty of Mary toward men in no way obscures or diminishes this unique mediation of Christ, but rather shows his power. For all the salvific influence of the Blessed Virgin on men originates, not from some inner necessity, but from divine pleasure and from the super-abundance of the merits of Christ. It rests on his mediation, depends on it, and draws all its power from it. In no way does it impede, but rather it fosters the immediate union of the faithful with Christ.
>
> *Constitution on the Church*, #60

Franciscans are devoted to Mary as a part of their heritage. But they do not spend more time on private revelations and devotions than they do on the gospels. We know that our faith does not require us to believe revelations given to private individuals. But the message of the gospel must be embraced wholeheartedly. Like Francis, Franciscans will maintain a faith-full balance in devotion to Mary. Most especially, their lives shall reflect her example of faith and love; of dedication and commitment even when it leads to a cross. Mary shall lead us to prayer and reflective pondering of the will of the Father. Mary will lead us to the service of our brothers and sisters. Like Mary, we too shall walk in the valley of darkness and the cross. But like her, we shall be present to know of the resurrection and prayerfully thank the Lord for both cross and resurrection. Particular devotions to Mary may come and go in the course of history. But the fundamental devotion of Franciscans to the Mother of God shall always be constant.

> . . . It (Vatican II) earnestly exhorts theologians and preachers of the divine word to abstain both from all false exaggerations as well as from too great narrowness of mind in considering the singular dignity of the Mother of God . . . Let the Faithful remember, moreover, that true devotion consists neither in sterile or transitory affection, nor in certain vain credulity, but proceeds from true faith, by which we are led to know the excellence of the Mother of God, and are moved to a filial love toward our Mother and to the imitation of her virtues.
>
> *Constitution on the Church*, #66 - 67

The example of St Francis serves us well. He was a man of faith, as Mary was a woman of faith. He was a man ready to absorb the gospels and make them his way of life. Mary was one who responded to her Son and the Father with wholehearted embrace of whatever Father or Son asked of her. Francis not only spoke about faith and hope and love but also implemented these qualities into his personal way of living. Mary is an example that often led him on to this achievement. Francis took time to pray, often going apart to stand still before God. Mary is a prime example of a prayerful person in touch with Yahweh.

As we try to follow Francis' way of life, his lifestyle, we too shall need faith and hope and love. We too must pray and stand still before God. We too must embrace the will of the Father. We too must be his messengers to our world. "May it be done to me according to your word."

16. From Assisi With Love

MOST FRANCISCANS HAVE THE TEMPTATION to give a conclusive study of the spirit of St Francis. Praise the Lord no one has yet been able to box that spirit in and package it. It is too fresh and new for that. But we still go on trying to add something to understanding the spirit of the little man from Assisi. My words are simply an addition to many more profound works. I claim no definitive conclusions, only my own ideas about the spirit of Francis. I would hope that all Franciscans would keep the door of their minds and hearts open to an ever deepening understanding of the spirit of this man of Assisi. Francis is always up-to-date, always relevant. because he dealt with basic human needs which remain constant.

The organizational principle which leads from Benedict through Dominic and Ignatius to the newer communities seems to have practically exhausted its inner possibilities. That, of course, does not mean that it could ever become superfluous or replaceable. But the fundamental newness which is precisely the thing being sought today by countless souls and in countless attempts at innovation, is to be found only along a completely different line; along the line of the original idea of Francis. In other words; in the direction of a freely chosen lifestyle and freely chosen bonds of love; in the direction of a life that operates through spontaneous initiative of the self rather than through great

constructs of the will; in the direction of a truly living
and individual personality shaped by its own inner laws
and standards. If God should some day deign to reveal
the Order of the future to his Church, the Order so
longingly sought by many of our best people, it will
surely bear the stamp of Francis' soul and spirit.
Living our future, von Galli S.J., 17

This very up-to-date aspect of Francis' spirit makes it
difficult to isolate one thing that pinpoints the spirit of
Francis. The search to discover such an ideal in Francis never
really ends. It is something that not only calls for intellectual
understanding but also for the experience of living in order
to be initiated into his life and spirit. No book can do all of
that. The Franciscan way of life is an adventure to be lived
and not simply something to be studied privately in one's
room. It requires following the gospel without watering it
down to suit one's own tastes. Like Francis, we will need to
accept our Father totally and without any hesitancy because
of fears of the consequences. We will accept the condescension of a so-called sophisticated society that cannot understand or accept such open hearted acceptance of the
Father's will. Our way may appear foolish to others and be a
source of some humiliations for us. But it is a world of
gospel-childlikeness that is responsive and delighted with the
Father's way of doing things. Ours is a world of practicality,
a world of mortgage payments and educational financing
while we work to free ourselves from making money the most
important thing in life. We want to be truly poor and we
struggle with the paradox (conflict?) of poverty and financial
security. We wonder about our loyalty and trust in God and
how we will respond when we are called to be a faith-full
people in a hopeless situation. We do not want to hurt
others, yet we must sometimes confront them so that they
may grow. Then we may have to accept insults and misunderstanding of our motives and still go on seeking to love

them and to show it. In the face of suffering, especially in others whom we love, we are often helpless. The Father will ask us to be patiently present without always knowing what to do. The gospel life is full of paradox. The paradox of our anger at the indifference of others who ought to know better and yet the love that reaches out to meet their every need. It is the reaching out to help others in their pain and being ready to accept their love when we are the suffering ones. It is throwing aside a dependency on things and yet begging for things so that others may not be in want. It is the paradox of learning the reality that we must die in order to live in Christ.

The way of Francis is the gospel way and it is the way of paradox. Sometimes this way seems complicated with all of its demands. Yet there is a simplicity about it that attracts something within us. One alone matters, Jesus Christ. He leads us to the Father. So that we may live the gospel life, He sends his Spirit into our hearts and the Trinity makes its home in us. We become family with this God who is Three-in-one. Jesus shows us his way through his revelation in Scripture and through his living body, the Church. His Word comes to us again and again. Over and over we will need to respond, ploughing the soil of our lives so that the seed of the word may take root there. There is challenge in that. There is sometimes a deep sense of our own littleness. But always, for Franciscans, there is the hope of personal conversion every day of our life. A hope based on our faith in Jesus Christ, our Lord, our Savior and our Brother.

The Franciscan way of life is not just another organization that you add to your list of 'clubs.' It is not simply a fraternal society that initiates you and then leaves you be so long as you pay your dues. The Franciscan way of life requires your life! It requires opening the deepest recesses of your heart to the Lord in the spirit of Francis of Assisi. Franciscans not only take their reading of the gospel seriously, they are serious about putting it into flesh-and-bone practice in their own lives. Francis wanted nothing else but to live the gospel. He listened to the word and lived it as he understood it at that moment. This was the 'gospel truth' for him. As Franciscans we become more and more sensitive to that word of God; we listen more intently; we reflect more constantly; we live it more consistently. Every nook and corner of our life is gradually opened to the word of the Lord. The power of the gospel in the life of Francis is made clear in this simple incident:

> What you speak of, Bernard, is something so great and wondrous that on it we ought to seek counsel from our Lord Jesus Christ and ask him to please show us his will in it and teach us how we can put it into practice. So, let us go together to the Bishop or to some good priest and we will have him say Mass. Then we will remain in prayer . . . asking God to show us on a three-fold opening of the missal what it pleases him to have us choose.

On opening the book, the first three words were:

> "If you wish to be perfect, go and sell everything you have, and give it to the poor."
> "Take nothing with you on the way."
> "Whoever wishes to follow me, let him deny himself . . ."

Francis exclaimed:

> That is what I want, that is what I am looking for, that is what I long to do with my inmost heart.
>
> *Words of St Francis*, #38 & 39

This is not magic at work nor some sort of simplistic approach to problems. This is an action of faith in Jesus and readiness to accept his word.

One element in the Franciscan spirit is the spirit of being poor. It is a deep, interior poverty that leads to joy in the Spirit. Francis was radical in his conversion. To be radical means to "put roots down." Francis put his roots down in the fertile soil of the gospel because it was Jesus' word to us. The spirit of the gospel permeated his life and his perspective on life. He was willing to be a seed that could grow and produce fruit only if it were buried in the soil of this gospel. There is no beating-around-the-bush in Francis. The gospel is his rule of life.

His awareness of the power of the gospel and his willingness to follow the gospel came to him not only in the soltidue of prayer on Mt Alverna but also in the delights of a "Brother Sun" dancing on the plains and valleys of Umbria. Francis knew joy because he freely put aside the baggage of life that might possess him and hold him back from God. If he were to possess monasteries, he would need men to protect them. To possess a place is to root oneself to that spot and to lose the gospel freedom. Once freed from possessiveness the whole world became 'his' since it belonged to the Father. All of this did not happen simply or magically for Francis. He struggled to come to such a point of freedom. Often his desire for solitude to think things through was denied him. He struggled with the "Martha and Mary" problem in his own life, deeply attracted to contemplation yet aware that the needs of others ought to be met. He accepted the direction that the Lord gave him in this search, difficult though it may have been for him. In this 'handing over,' this 'yielding' to the Lord he found joy.

. . . But one is probably justifiably insistent in maintaining that genuine Franciscan joy cannot carry heavy personal luggage if it is to give its open embrace to the poor of the earth. Our Blessed Father objected that to have property would necessitate having weapons to defend it, and there are obvious present analogies. Who has not seen the little pistols of irritability and the hand-granades of petulance with which a religious will defend his small citadel of supposed needs, conveniences and arrangements? St Francis wandered over the earth after the manner of a young heir inspecting with satisfaction his Father's property. And that is just what he was. He never needed to grasp things. For he had really understood that in having nothing, he possessed all things, and that whatever he needed would be given him in that hour.

Marginals, Sister Mary Francis, 72

The spirit of Franciscan poverty brings us to a delight in the gladness of today. Today is the road to the future. Yesterday has brought us to where we are. But we can act and love and forgive and show compassion only in the 'todays' of our life. Francis chose to live in those todays on his path to the dreams of all our tomorrows.

Francis experienced the hard road of failure and the unexpected expectations of the Father. As a young man he sought to become a knight. He never quite made it. His tastes were fastidious and he disliked unpleasant things, especially anything like the smell and touch of lepers. He came to embrace lepers and wash their wounds. He leaned to solitude and contemplation on the Alvernas of his life. The gospel called him from the mountain to serve the people who walked in the valley of life. He loved the Lady Clare with a deep and lasting love. But he eased from personal contact with her. He sought out the loneliest places, the poor huts of Rivo Torto, and the sign of his own poverty. Yet he accepted the gift of a mountain called Alverna from a good friend. He was deeply aware of the scandalous lives of many prelates in the Church and how they brought harm to the Church through their lack of faith. Yet he remained a person who deeply respected authority and those who celebrated Mass. He tried with all his energy to keep the inner vision of gospel-living alive in his Order. Yet he experienced the agony of seeing his dream watered down to suit the convenience and comfort of miserly-spirited men who called themselves his followers. Francis, who delighted in the beauties of God's creation and praised them in his Canticle of Brother Sun, eventually went blind and could not see these wonders any longer. Clearly, Francis understood from experience the consequences of following Jesus and his gospel message. "Deny yourself; come after me; take up your cross."

The poverty of Francis was not imposed, it was embraced. To embrace this Lady Poverty it is necessary to approach her with arms that are empty and free. But even more is required. The embrace will be sincere not simply because our arms are empty and we freely choose to embrace the Lady, but also because the heart is full of love for the Lady. This inner embrace of poverty, this letting loose of self for the sake of Jesus is at the heart of the spirit of Francis. How gently Francis reveals the need for open hands and a full heart is shown in the story of perfect joy that he shares with Brother Leo. The rejection, the non-acceptance by one's own brothers becomes a symbolic way of expressing the completeness with which Francis wished to be clay in the hands of the Divine Potter.

> Brother Leo, were it to please God that the lesser Brothers gave in every country a grand example of holiness and edification in virtue, nevertheless write it down and take careful note of it: there is not perfect joy in that.

> O Brother Leo, though a lesser brother give sight to the blind, straighten the limbs of the crippled, drive out demons, give hearing to the deaf, make the lame walk, give speech to the mute and still more, raise up the four-day dead, write down that there is not perfect joy in that.

O Brother Leo, if a lesser Brother knew all the languages and all the sciences and all the Scriptures, so that he could prophesy and reveal not only things future but also the secrets of consciences and minds, write that perfect joy lies not in that.

If we get to St Mary's of the Angels so drenched with rain and frozen with cold and spattered with mud and afflicted with hunger, and knock at the door of the place and the porter comes in anger and says: "Who are you?" and we say: "We are two of your brothers." And if he says: "You are not telling the truth, you are rather two loafers who are going about fooling the world and robbing the alms of the poor—get out!" and he does not open the door for us, and makes us stay outdoors in the snow and rain amid the cold and our hunger, till nightfall; then if we endure all those insults and cruelties and rebuffs patiently and without being ruffled or murmuring at him and we humbly and charitably think that this porter really knows us but that God is having him talk up to us that way; Oh, Brother Leo, write that there is perfect joy in that.

And if we go on knocking, and he comes out all wrought up and drives us away with abusive language and cuffs us as if we were impudent clods, saying: "Get out of here you low-down, thievish fellows, go on to the hostel, for you will get neither bite nor bed here." If we take that patiently, with good cheer and charity; Oh, Brother Leo, write that therein there is perfect joy.

And if we, still forced by hunger, cold and the darkness, go on rapping and asking for the love of God amid many tears that he should open and let us in and he, more enraged than before, says: "Now these fellows are impudent oafs, and I am going to pay them out as they deserve!" And he comes out with knotted cudgel, grabs us by the cowl, flings us on the ground, rolls us about in the snow, and beats us joint by joint with that cudgel; if we took all this punishment patiently and with good cheer, thinking of it as the suffering of Christ the blessed one which we ought to bear for his love; Oh, Brother Leo, write down that therein is perfect joy.

And now listen to the conclusion, Brother Leo. Above all the graces and gifts of the Holy Spirit which Christ grants to his friends, there is that of overcoming themselves and gladly, for the love of Christ, bearing pain, insults, disgrace, and discomfort, because we cannot glory in any of the other gifts of God—they are not ours but God's. Therefore the Apostle says: "What have you that you have not received from God? And if you have received it from God, why do you glory as if you had not received it?"

But in the cross of tribulation and affliction we may glory because that is our due, and so the Apostle says: "I do not wish to glory in anything but in the cross of our Lord Jesus Christ." To whom ever be honor and glory, world without end, Amen.

Words of St Francis, #18

Perfect joy is connected with the cross. Francis is not being eccentric nor unreal in what he shared with Brother Leo. The implications of this story demand a dying to oneself that is not simply a sentimental sort of "Alleluia" stemming from a 'beautiful' experience of God's love. It lays our life on the line for the Lord even when we are treated unjustly, unfairly and with an anger that we did not create. It allows us to maintain an inner peace in such situations and still be willing to accept the Brother whose cudgel puts bumps on our head. It brings us in silence before accusers without having to 'prove' ourselves; but to leave the judgement in the hands of our Father and continue to give witness to gospel understanding, forgiveness, compassion and love. It goes counter to much of our ordinary way of thinking, but it is the gospel way. Someone has written of the Franciscan Order that it is: "An Order without order. A miracle of divine providence. In spite of it we not only live, but thrive." When we willingly take Jesus at his word even apparent failure cannot hinder our pilgrimage to the Lord and his kingdom.

Franciscans are a people free to move ahead because we are not tied to one particular way of responding to the gospel. We are free to be real and laugh at ourselves even while we are dead serious about the way we seek to serve the Lord. We are free of excess baggage or of being possessed by possessions and yet absolutely delighted with the things the Father provides for us. We are the poorest of the poor, recognizing how meager is our response to the lavish love of the Father, yet we are ready to share our meager riches with others. We are new fools for Christ, ready and willing to accept blame or praise with equal poise because either can bring us closer to the Father. We will accept the perfect joy of suffering for the sake of Jesus because He has told us that his way would also include the cross. We do not seek it. It is simply one consequence of taking the gospel seriously. Whatever the gospel brings to us will be OK for it will bring us to identification with the Father. The Franciscan way of life may include conflict and problems, but we shall work to transform barriers into bridges through the spirit of Francis of Assisi.

It is possible that this sort of approach to life will be seen as foolishness and eccentricity. Francis is just a nicely unique individual who does such strange things as talking about perfect joy, but no one can seriously follow such off-beat ideas. Perhaps such a feeling reveals where we are in our own seriousness about living the gospel. Yet, despite this vague,

uneasy feeling we may have about getting over our heads
with Francis, he still pulls at our desire for joy.

> Actually, however, a certain eccentricity, a disturbance
> of the equilibrium that we call 'normal' can indeed, and,
> in my opinion, will in fact, show up in the person's
> natural disposition. God's grace latches on to this in
> order to carry the person beyond himself. Certainly
> this eccentricity can just as well degenerate into self-
> complacency, excessive pride, brutal egoism. But when
> it flows into service to fellowmen, into devotedness and
> self-forgetfulness, then it is precisely this extraordinari-
> ness, tamed and yet not rigid, harmonious and yet
> eccentric, that is the sign of the divine. Not that the
> extraordinary in itself amounts to that—rather the
> extraordinariness of the extraordinary does. That is to
> say, although there is dissonance, there is also harmony!
> although there is distortion, there is also balance;
> although there is ruin, there is also constructive effort.
> That is something a person can perhaps taste or savor.
> But he cannot calculate it . . .
>
> *Living our future*, von Galli, 30

There are times when we are misled in our efforts to
understand a saint. If we were to look only at the significant
and obvious events in Francis' life to show his living of the
gospel, we might come away discouraged. Most of us have
few really vitally significant things happen to us. Life is very
ordinary. What is more important is to search for the thread
that ties life together. In Francis, that thread is his consistent
response to the will of the Father as he understood it at any
given moment. It springs from the bonding between Francis
and Jesus that found its plan in the gospel. As Francis
understood the gospel better, he also tried to live it more
effectively. Change was the result of allowing the gospel to
be *thee* way to live and knowing and loving Jesus as *thee* way

to the Father. Then the unexpected call of the Father to explore new heights was a natural part of life and not a new threat to it. You and I will follow such a path if we choose the way of Francis, for the unexpected then becomes the 'normal' for us and we become good witnesses of the gospel way of life.

> . . . Society asks us with particular insistence these days to give an account of ourselves. But the account men really demand is that we show ourselves persons who know God intimately, live for him utterly, and are thus able to make the reality of the living God 'come alive' for them also. They have every right to demand this account of us, and we have every duty to respond. It was the way of St Francis to speak to men simply, and always more by the calibre of his life than by his words, of a God he knew and loved and lived for. It was thus that he brought back to a languid and sensual society the enthusiasm and joy of the children of God.
>
> *Marginals*, Sister Mary Francis, 18

For us to be such witnesses requires us to be free of preconceived ideas of what the gospel says. It may require scraping off years of accumulated complacency in our response to Jesus' word. It requires seeking Lady Poverty and embracing the emptying out that she will require of us. The frills, the time that is wasted on arguments about externals (all by themselves), the resistence to walk a different way than we have grown accustomed to, the judging and condemning of others in preference to our own conversion—all such things must go! In return the Spirit shall truly be free to operate in our lives. His gifts will be loosened from rusty mis-use to well-oiled and sensitive use. With delight we will fling our hats in the air and be ready to be a fool for Christ and enjoy every moment of it. We will be a people whose hope and trust in the Father cannot be dampened by even the worst of calamities nor by the seemingly insurmountable world problems that surround us. Somehow, somewhere, there is a place for us to do what the Lord requires and we shall continue to be a people whose hope brings hope to others. We shall be like the man in this little parable:

A man lay on the grass gazing at the sky. He saw balloons and birds flying about in a celestial ballet. Red and green and pink and orange balloons. Balloons of bright yellow and blue and gold. Finches and cardinals and bluejays and sparrows flew in and out among the balloons in a dancing pattern of delight. Bright sunlight filtered through and around the balloons.

Then suddenly there was a riot of bursting balloons and cackling birds as boys with BB guns pelted them. Birds fell in the grass, stunned by the BB's. In what seemed a moment and an eternity, the sky was empty and it was deathly quiet.

Now the boys were gone; the balloons were gone; the birds were gone. Nothing but the memory of them remained for the man on the grass. Scattered remnants of rubber still drifted in the quiet air. The man was alone.

"Is this how dreams die?" he pondered. "Is this the suddenness that strikes at the dreams and ambition of men? Is all our seeking and searching to end like this?"

Even as he spoke a large yellow balloon floated into sight followed by a red one and a bright orange one. He sprang up and looked around. All he saw was a man in a brown robe, red-faced from blowing up balloons and lofting them in the air. The little brown-robed man was delighted as he watched them drift upward and out of reach. He absorbed their colors in his sparkling eyes.

The man on the grass stopped short. His reverie had been interrupted. But did this brown-robed man have the answer to his questions? What is done is done. But we can make what will be!

We Franciscans must be ready to delight in blowing up balloons. We stand ready to replace the love the world has lost, not with our own meager love, but with the love of Christ that lives in us. We have chosen to identify with Jesus through the eccentric, the poor, the balloon-blowing Francis. We need not run to some leper colony in order to imitate Francis' work with lepers. There are enough lepers available right at hand who need our care and offer us the opportunity of loving them and being loved in return. We may not find a cave on a mountain hillside in which to pray and agonize over our conversion. But the inner cave of our heart will face that same struggle that Francis faced in his cave. We may not have the imagination nor ability to play a violin with no more than a couple of sticks, but we shall stretch our spirit so that the dream of the gospel finds room in our life. We shall often be without answers to the problems we or others may face. But we shall face them nonetheless and walk together in living them through to their ending.

It is not so much what Francis did that we need to do, as it is who Francis was that we need to be. He was so realistic because he was so simple. He was so simple because he believed God. In an age that loves above all to look at itself in a hand mirror and whisper: "How adult!" it may cause some squirming on chairs and polite coughing behind hands to touch on the subject of childlikeness. Yet a sophisticated spirituality will stub its pedicured toes not only on Francis, but on

Christ. "Unless you be converted and become as little children." (Mt 18:3)

One evidence of spiritual adulthood is the capacity for becoming like a child. It is a very difficult business to become as a little child, taking God at his word, believing our Father, trusting the will which we cannot fathom, understanding—among other things—that it is only love that will effect any kind of renewal in anything.

Francis was a hard realist. That is why he was so great a poet. He never escaped down words or even ideas, but pursued them to an ultimate meaning. The dreamer-saint of Assisi was a man of such action as to happily upset a whole European society by his humble presence. Like all great dreamers, he got things moving. In fact, he got things done—and by the very simple expedient of doing them. He was first of all himself what he invited others to be. Surely there is no need to discuss Francis' witness to Christ in the Church before all the people of God. It is not a matter of the means of giving witness which he chose. He simply was himself a witness by his personal holiness.

Marginals, Sister Mary Francis 15 - 17 - 18

Like a rhapsody, poverty and joy repeat themselves in the life of Francis. Francis described his Lady Poverty in the manner in which a knight might speak of his Lady-love. For Francis, Lady Poverty was a lady more real than any flesh and blood Lady. In his mind the Lady Poverty must be served with honor and loving respect. She is treated with tenderness and affection. Perhaps only dreamers can understand this dream Lady of Francis. But she dominates his thoughts and directs much of what his spirit seeks to express. His praise of Lady Poverty is beautiful to read and concludes with these words of affection and joy:

> Lord Jesus, show me the paths of your dearly beloved
> poverty . . . Poverty clung to you so faithfully that she
> began her service to you in the very womb of your
> mother, where you had of all living bodies the tiniest.
> Then too, as you came forth from the womb, she wel-
> comed you to the holy manger and the stable, and as
> you went about in the world, she kept you so despoiled
> of everything that she had you without a place to rest
> your head.

> Yes, when, because the cross was so high, your very
> Mother—and such a Mother—could not reach you . . .
> then, I say, Lady Poverty was there like a most welcome
> handmaiden with all her privations to enfold you more
> tightly than ever and to share the more feelingly in your
> torment.

> Oh, who would not love this, your Lady Poverty, above
> all others. I entreat you for the favor of being sealed
> with this privilege, I crave to be enriched with this
> treasure. I beg you, O Jesus most poor, that it may be
> the distinction of me and mine forevermore, for your
> name's sake to possess nothing under heaven as our own
> and to be sustained as long as our poor flesh lives, only
> with the closely restricted use of things given us by
> others.

Words of St Francis, #16

Francis is a poet and uses a poet's vision in speaking about
the Lady Poverty. He gives her shape and form and attributes
to her an intimacy with Jesus. He calls the Lady Poverty his
very own Lady. She is the Lady who embraces the Lord and
identifies with Jesus in every nook and cranny of his life. In
suffering and in health, in hunger and abundance, in joy and

pain, in acceptance by others or in rejection, the Lady Poverty remains constant in her love for Jesus. Whatever price the gospel way of life may bring, Franciscans shall accept and embrace the Lady Poverty's demands. If death or desertion enters the life of a Franciscan, he remains faithful even in the face of death. The beautiful, poetic Lady embodies the dream of Francis to belong completely to the Lord in every instance of life and in every place the Lord may lead.

This deep readiness to allow Jesus full reign in our lives will bring us to joy. There is a quiet, inner spot in our hearts that is certain of Jesus. Surrounded by events that may threaten or challenge, the followers of Francis maintain calmness because the Lord is with them. He said he would be and he is. We can delight in some of the stories about Francis, about preaching to birds or calmly walking into the camp of the Sultan. In each case it is a natural thing to do according to the circumstance. There is a calm acceptance of blindness and the pain he suffered from the Stigmata, because they bring him to the Lord who loves him. We will walk in the joy and wonder of God's creations that gave birth to the Canticle of Brother Sun and find ourselves led to the crucible of God's love on a cross. We listen to Francis speak of the gospel life and wonder at the fact of dying in order to live, and now we find ourselves willing to let loose of self-seeking in order to live in the Spirit. Yet, it is easy to slip away from commitment when it seems to demand too much of us. We know the kind of joy Francis came to, but we are sometimes unsure of our own ability to believe with his kind of faith. The important thing about our promise to follow Francis is that we try to keep it, even when we break it. Even while we are uncertain about this poverty business, Francis shows us his empty pockets and assures us that we will make it all right. While we plead for more time to make up our mind, Francis reminds us that "time's a wastin' " while we're doing all this thinking. No good Franciscan will try to corral you into our way of life or use sensitivity sessions to capture you. Your decision must be free and honest, and it must be your decision to follow this gospel centered way of life. Your decision is to be clear-headed and warm-hearted. But we want to walk with you and be poor with you and bring you joy no matter what. We want you to experience shalom in your life and we will do what we can to help you achieve it. We want you to forget yourself and be surprised by the fulfillment that comes to someone who learns what real love is all about.

It requires considerable imaginational gymnastics to picture St Francis pondering his personal fulfillment. He was, for one thing, too busy. Like all the saints he became a perfectly fulfilled person, but it is a safe wager that he never once in his religious life gave a thought to personal fulfillment. True personal fulfillment is a natural phenomonen of sacrificial love, which occurs, not a course of action which has to be planned.

Marginals, Sister Mary Francis, 88

Here at the heart of Franciscan poverty is the realization of how important self-acceptance can be. When we are self conscious; when our concern is with how we appear to others; when we cannot admit to mistakes because of feelings of insecurity; when we must dominate in order to avoid confrontation; when we withdraw from life for fear of making a mistake; when we need to keep so occupied that we avoid any real solitude—then we will not be able to live our Franciscan life to the hilt. All of us are working to become better Franciscans. It is the work of a lifetime and not a weekend. Our freedom will allow us to experience the joy of appreciating all things and people, for Jesus has promised us light and life and joy. As we grow in poverty we begin to understand that problems do not destroy perfection but provide opportunities for new growth. We embrace life and live it until we die, knowing that the power of the Spirit shall bring us to the perfection we seek. We walk with Jesus to the Father as did Francis. The dark valleys of life make us more aware of the good Shepherd who removes the fear of the dark by his own light. The experience of the presence of the Father who loves us shall bring us to wanting to set up tents to dwell here forever. The spirit of St Francis, unboxed and as free as ever, shall lead us to full confidence in the Father which shall lead us to independence of things and leave us free to share life with God's people which shall in turn bring glory to the Father whose power works in us. It all depends on our God, on Father, Son and Spirit entering and taking hold of us and bringing us to themselves.

> But God is rich in mercy; because of his great love for us he brought us to life with Christ when we were dead in sin. By this favor you were saved. Both with and in Christ Jesus he raised us up and gave us a place in the heavens, that in the ages to come he might display the great wealth of his favor, manifested by his kindness to us in Christ Jesus. I repeat, it is owing to his favor that salvation is yours through faith. This is not your own doing, it is God's gift; neither is it a reward for anything you have accomplished, so let no one pride himself on it. We are truly his handiwork, created in Christ Jesus to lead the life of good deeds which God prepared for us in advance.
>
> Ephesians 2: 4 - 10

The spirit of Francis shall brush the 20th century with its freshness as fully as it did the 13th century. There is no way to hem it in or confine it. Francis was a man in love. Lovers do not count pennies nor measure the gift of self in miserly terms. Francis still shows us the vigor that God's love can bring to a man and through him to a tired, disillusioned world. Today, we are not trying to go backwards to the 13th century, but rather to take the spirit of Francis and transfuse today's world with it. Francis scattered the seed of God's word to his world, our job is the same. Nothing can stop us. No earthly power; no amount of bickering; no persecution can still the power of the gospel. Like Francis, we are on the move through God's world stretching ahead to the fullness of the kingdom. There is a motion here and a movement that cannot be stilled or quieted. For there will always be those who capture the spirit of Francis and make it alive for today.

> The eager face under the brown hood was that of a man always going somewhere, as if he followed as well as watched the flight of the birds. And this sense of motion is indeed the meaning of the whole revolution that he made; for the work that has now to be described was of the nature of an earthquake or a volcano, an explosion that drove outwards with dynamic energy the forces stored up by ten centuries in the monastic fortress or arsenal and scattered all its riches recklessly to the ends of the earth.

> . . . it is true to say that what St Benedict has stored, St Francis scattered; but in the world of spiritual things, what had been stored into barns like grain, was scattered over the world as seed. The servants of God who had been a beseiged garrison became a marching army; the ways of the world were filled as with thunder with the trampling of their feet, and far ahead of that ever swelling host went a man singing, as simply as he had sung that morning in the winter woods, where he walked alone.
>
> *St Francis of Assisi*, G.K. Chesterton, 98

No matter where you hear this call, no matter what your position or dignity, no matter how great or small your ability may be, the call to follow Francis will turn you into a person who spreads the seeds of the gospel wherever you go. It will not really matter if you see all the fruit that the seed produces, but only that you are lavish in sowing. It is not always up to you to finish the task, but neither are you free to desist from it. The gospel way of life shall burn within your human heart and forever warm you and push you to warm others. Little by little, explosion by explosion, the power within shall deprive you of everything so that you may possess Him who alone is everything. Whether we are welcomed or rejected, living or dying, sorrowing or joyful, we shall march in the security of the Father's love. When Sister Death finally calls us through the final dying that leads to unending life, it shall be like the picture painted by the words of Chesterton:

> While it was yet twilight a figure appeared silently and suddenly on a little hill above the city, dark against the fading darkness. For it was the end of a long and stern night, a night of vigil, not unvisited by stars. He stood with his hands lifted, as in so many statues and pictures; and about him was a burst of birds singing; and behind him was the break of day.
>
> *St Francis of Assisi*, G.K. Chesterton, 36 - 37

17. If You Take My Hand

THE QUALITY OF OUR FRANCISCAN-CHRISTIAN LIFE shall require many virtues. A few of them bear further reflection.

We have already spoken about the fact that Franciscans are expected to be a people of hope. This quality will mark the person who possesses it as someone different Many people are predicting a gloom-and-doom future that looks really bad. Our earth, rich as it is, is not providing enough food for everyone—or perhaps we have not learned how to distribute an adequate food supply. Many means are sought to solve this problem, some that seem to go counter to good morality. We have a tinderbox situation of hatred between Jew and Arab and terrorist attacks in many parts of the world. Our own country lives with doors locked out of the fear of criminals. There is no lack of material for the gloom-and-doom people. However, after we list the litany of evils abroad in the world, we are still in need of a people who can bring hope to these situations. On the one hand, we are not looking for people who are foolishly optimistic and out of touch with reality, dreaming impossible dreams with no foundations for their dreams. Some people preach that man is so good that all we have to do is let him alone and we will come to peace and justice and joy. On the other hand we have the people who see man as evil and degraded. Nothing can change the downward trend that will eventually end in self-destruction. Again, events can lend support to either viewpoint if you look at them with an eye prejudiced in either direction.

Once again we need the common sense of a Francis. We are sinners. We are called to be saints. We can and do sin, but God calls us out of sinfulness into his own wonderful light. This fact of sin and sainthood creates a tension in us. We experience the temptation to sin even while we are aware of our call to holiness. We are in conflict about how to implement the gospel when we can't seem to satisfy the human needs around us, even our own. To help a neighbor tonight limits my ability to help someone else who needs help tonight. When we listen seriously to the Word of the Lord, we will find this tension in ourselves. The common sense of Francis leads us to the course that opens our life to living this gospel and allowing the tension to move us toward holiness. It tells us that we are sinners striving to become saints. We have not yet arrived. Forgetting the past, we stretch toward the future by dealing 'gospelly' with the present. One important function of the Word of God in the Bible is to allow us to see ourselves in our failures as well as to call us to conversion. The quality of hope will flow from the quality of our relationship to Jesus in faith.

Hope is not "pie in the sky when you die" sort of thing. It is not a tool to be clung to when everything else fails. Neither is it simply the opposite of despair. We have often boxed hope up into these kinds of definitions. But they are far too limited to be the reality of hope. Hope is passionately positive and is an eager quality of the Franciscan whether despair is on the horizon or not. Hope does not imagine there is a way out! Hope *knows* there is a way out. Whatever the situation may be, however great the problem may be, however helpless a person may be, hope can and ought to be present. For hope is not something that is dependent on our power and wisdom. Hope depends on Jesus; Hope relies on the Father; Hope is a response to the presence of the Holy Spirit. The foundation for hope is the fact that God loves me. I believe that with all my heart and soul and mind and strength. That being so, he will not abandon me nor his people to destruction. So no matter what the situation may be, my Father will care for me and bring life through the situation. That is the foundation for hope. Even though a solution is not found at any given moment, hope allows me the strength to face whatever is happening as a call to greater intimacy with my Father. Hence, the hopeful person is not the person with all the answers. Rather, he has only one answer: There is the seed of promise in every situation because my Father loves me. That is reality!

Hope does not come easily when we have grown used to being independent. We have been taught the importance of being self-sufficient. The gospel idea of hope requires us to free ourselves from the perspective of this absolute kind of independence. It draws us to a realistic dependence on God. Obviously, this sort of faith-dependence goes counter to much of what society teaches as success. It is not worldly wisdom to rely so totally on God. However, even the worldly wise ought to be able to see where such independent thinking has brought us. It may be fine for making profits, but it does little for the happiness of the human heart. Each of us fights against the abandonment that hope requires. We need Jesus to free us from this self seeking. Were we to rely solely on our own power to achieve hope, we would meet with frustration. We need God and we need to acknowledge that fact. Hope cannot leave God out of the picture because God is the foundation for our hope. Father Bernard Haring C.SS.R. begins his book on hope by writing about a vision he had of a Universal Congress of Skunks. Presiding at the opening session was the supervisor of Devils, a Super-Skunk who addressed the congress in these words:

> Over the past few months and years, you have been doing very poorly in terms of stinking and radiating frustration around you. You seem unable to cope with the challenge of that old guy, John XXIII, who should have died some years earlier instead of spreading

optimism about the world. So far, you stupid Devils have offered the whole world nothing but naked pessimism which is no longer a marketable product. You must concoct a more effective mixture as suggested by today's chemists.

. . . Availing yourself of all your gifts of oratory, preach faith, but let it be a faith without hope, consisting of formulas, a mere catalog of things and beliefs; this will be one of our new gimmicks.

. . . Devote considerable attention to progressives, encouraging them to expend at least 90% of their energy on fighting conservatives, whether they be bishops, theologians, canonists, nuns or holy people. Teach everybody to pray along with Charles de Gaulle at Montmarte: "Sacred Heart of Jesus, trust in me!" Tell believers to have faith in themselves; let them forget the grace of God.

Let priests and nuns talk day and night about optional celibacy, but rightly understood as optional fidelity. . . . Make a great show of conservatives whose charism is to frustrate progressives. Incite progressives to display even more bitterness than those already frustrated by reforms. In all this be utterly shameless; claim that you are acting in the best interest of religion or faith or piety; you will then have a potent mixture at your disposal.

Piously insist on the observance of all commandments save that of love and mercy . . . Be wary of any method advocating love and concern for other people. Be voluble about Christian hope but avoid any mention of Christ's death and resurrection as the basis of hope. Never bring into play such old-fashioned notions as self-denial; speak only about an easily accessible hope, a man-made hope, a secular hope for earthly progress.

Do not tolerate a sense of humor for it could be fatal because of its relationship to humility; present humor solely as a waste of time. Encourage only a futile optimism based on secular achievements or pietistic magic.

Hope is the remedy, Bernard Haring, 15ff

Our hope is built solidly on God, but especially on the fact of his Son's passion, death and resurrection. How often St Paul tells us that our hope for future life comes from this source. If Christ is not raised from the dead, our faith, our hope are meaningless. Should we base hope on technological progress alone we might have no problem reaching the moon but our hearts will still be empty. Our Father keeps his word. We trust him.

Francis of Assisi was a man of hope. Once he had made his faith-filled decision to follow the gospel, his hope was boundless. There was in Francis a total acceptance of Jesus and his word. Jesus said clearly that the birds of the air are cared for by the Father but that people were more important than birds. Francis believed that the Father would care for him. Jesus said that he and the Father would come to believers and make their home with them. Francis believed that God was present within him. Jesus taught that the Father runs to a wayward son to offer forgiveness and to embrace that son. Francis believed that the Father runs to Francis to forgive and embrace him as his son. Jesus promised that the poor and gentle of heart would see God and experience his presence. Francis handed himself over to the Father and experienced the joy of his presence. Jesus taught that those who follow him must leave behind whatever one possessed and follow him. Francis did just that. Jesus said that to those who love him and serve him all things will work to their good. Francis believed this even when the human situation seemed to speak differently. Jesus prayed that his followers would be so intimately united that their unity would be a sign of their faith. Francis sought always to make his fraternity such a sign to the world. Jesus spoke of the cross as part of the way of doing the Father's will. Francis prayed to be identified with Jesus in suffering and in love. The hope that Francis shows us is not based on his own abilities nor even on his personal experiences. It is based on his faith-relationship to Jesus and the Father and the Spirit. With God, all things are possible, so Francis hoped for all things from God. Paul's words are a ringing challenge to us to grow in hope:

> We know that God makes all things work together for the good of those who have been called according to his decree. Those whom he foreknew he predestined to share the image of his Son, that the Son might be the first born of many brothers. Those he predestined he likewise called: those he called he also justified; and those he justified he in turn glorified. What shall we say after that? If God is for us, who can be against us? Is it possible that he who did not spare his own Son but handed him over for the sake of us all will not grant us all things besides? Who shall bring a charge against God's chosen ones? God, who justifies? Who shall condemn them? Christ Jesus, who died or rather was raised up, who is at the right hand of God and who intercedes for us?

> Who will separate us from the love of Christ? Trial, or distress, or persecution, or hunger, or nakedness, or danger, or the sword? As Scripture says: "For your sake we are being slain all the day long; we are looked upon as sheep to be slaughtered." Yet in all this we are more than conquerors because of him who has loved us. For

I am certain that neither death nor life, neither angels nor principalities, neither the present nor the future, nor powers, neither height nor depth nor any other creature, will be able to separate us from the love of God that comes to us in Christ Jesus, our Lord.

Romans 8: 28 - 39

In the lonely, precious moments of solitude on Mt Alverna, Francis expressed his absolute faith and hope in the simple words: "My God and my all." Hope holds nothing back. Hope takes the risks the Lord leads us to take. Hope is not afraid of seeming failure. Hope is not intimidated by seemingly insoluble problems. Hope plants herself firmly in the Lord, in the only reality that ultimately makes sense.

SISTER DEATH

Closely linked to the Christian's hope in Christ is his hope in life after death. Death is the doorway to life, a stepping-stone to perfect unity with God. What we begin on earth is continued and climaxed in heaven. The passageway from the one to the other is given the name of death.

Modern man seems to have many anxieties about death. Many simply refuse to think about it hoping that it will go away. Some see death only as a time for judgement when we will get what we deserve. To others it is a moment of sadness when loved ones are left behind. For those who are actually near death and aware of the presence of Sister Death, it can mean a happy delivery from pain and suffering. For us Franciscans death is a Sister, a friend.

The realistic facing of our personal death brings with it some very positive results. If we have been a people of faith, then we approach this idea with a feeling of calmness. But the realization of our personal death also helps us to be more honest in our evaluation of the kind of person we are, the importance of the things we are doing and the whole lifestyle that we are living.

God has made us free. We can choose the things we wish to do. We can decide the direction we want our lives to take. The significant point about freedom is not simply that we can change our minds but rather that we can make up our minds about the direction of our lives. We can decide to be kind and thus become a kind person. We can decide to be gentle and become a gentle person. Which is more than saying we are persons who do kind things. Our choices help to create the kind of person we become. Our decisions touch others and create the kind of world we live in. As free human beings we choose the way of life we will follow and act and decide according to such a basic decision.

There are many possibilities in this choosing. Life can mean different things. It can simply reflect an attitude of 'passing through-only-once-so-get-all-you-can' and pleasure can dominate our choices. It can develop from a philosophy that God does everything anyway so why worry about choices that we don't really have. Lifestyle can reflect the philosophy that winning is everything or that money is everything and I will choose and decide in such a way that I win and get more money. Anything that helps me win or gain profit is good. Whatever my fundamental choice may be, I expend energy, time and decision to achieve the dream of that fundamental choice. That becomes the thing that gives meaning to life.

The thought of death can throw a monkey wrench in all of this. Whatever my choice, death forces me to face the wisdom of that choice. We have only one lifetime to decide what direction our lives will take. Death reminds us of that. We know very well that 'things' are useless in the face of death. For the Christian, this realization makes a difference in the value that 'things' have in life. If life on earth is the time to get acquainted with the God who shall be intimate friend through eternity, then I choose the things or attitudes or bonds that will deepen my friendship with God. In death there is a finality about the choice we have made. While we live, we can always reverse our decisions, change our minds, be converted and live differently. In the new life after death there is no more changing because our choice is then finalized. We are caught up either in union with the Trinity or deprived of that union. We either experience an absolute wonder of acceptance and love or find ourselves deprived of it. Our lifetime decisions can make a great deal of difference in that final choice. The faithful reflection on death is a help in making wise choices for it keeps us from being satisfied with fringe service to the Lord. It brings us to the final reality, the ending of life. In that ending of life on earth we are better able to judge what is really important.

> While we live in our present tent we groan; we are weighed down because we do not wish to be stripped naked but rather to have the heavenly dwelling envelop us, so that what is mortal may be absorbed by life. God has fashioned us for this very thing and has given us the Spirit as a pledge of it.

> Therefore, we continue to be confident. We know that while we dwell in the body we are away from the Lord. We walk by faith, not by sight. I repeat, we are full of confidence and would much rather be away from the body and at home with the Lord. This being so, we make it our aim to please him whether we are with him or away from him. The lives of all of us are to be revealed before the tribunal of Christ so that each one may receive his recompense, good or bad, according to his life in the body.
>
> 2 Corinthians 5: 4 - 10

From the perspective of faith, reflection on death gives significance and direction to our daily decisions. Even the very ordinary, day-by-day decisions that we make take on meaning in the light of death. They reveal the direction of our lives. They say something about the values that we cherish. They tell us about who or what is important in our lives. Ignoring death is ignoring reality. But our reflection is neither morbid nor depressing. Quite the opposite, the reflection of the faith-full person brings new vitality to what I do and say today. I become more vitally interested in this earthly life that will bring me to life with the Father in heaven. Nothing is meaningless except the failure to evaluate and assess my decisions in the light of the moment when earthly life shall cease.

Stop for a moment to consider your own death. Obviously it may be sudden or the result of an illness. The Lord may come to you in the sacrament of the Sick to touch you with his strength and to bring you his healing peace. But here you are, face to face with your moment of death. You have chosen to follow the Franciscan way of life. You have tried to live a life of faith, hope and love. You have worked hard to make your life more reflective of the gospel of Jesus. You have sought to build solid friendships. You have tried to understand others; to forgive them; to be happy with them. You have tried to be among the little 'poor ones' to whom Christ is everything. You have experienced pain and hurt and prejudice. Misunderstanding and frustration have not been absent. You have had to live with problems you could not solve. You have failed the Lord and those you love by your lack of awareness or readiness to share. You have shared often with others—shared time, ability, and material wealth with those in need. You have been trustworthy and shared yourself in the fraternity and with all the people in your life. You have known weakness and failure, but you have refused to buckle under. You have tried to forgive friends who have failed you, even Franciscans who may have failed you in a time of need. Now your pilgrimage is about to end. Life is going to be transformed. We have lived for this moment and now we are coming home.

The experience of approaching death is a new one, so there may be some anxiety. But we know Jesus. We know his love and we know our faith-response to that love. We are not perfect, but we have never ceased trying to do better. So now, as our life on earth comes to an end, there is a quiet acceptance of this final moment of life. Jesus is with us. Even death cannot separate us from him. There is some sadness to move away for the moment from those we love. We have not finished everything we started. But those we love are in God's hands and that work can be done by others. Only sin would bring me sorrow now. I may not be able to pray well, but I trust the Spirit to pray for me. We shall know why we have lived.

Such is the death of a loyal Franciscan and Christian. St Francis saw it in this way as he sang out in the last verses of his Canticle of Brother Sun:

> All praise be yours, my Lord, through Sister Death, from whose embrace no mortal can escape. Woe to those who die in mortal sin! Happy those she finds doing her will. The second death can do no harm.

Among philosophers and theologians, many explanations are made about the meaning of death. Some say that as the body grows weak it can no longer support the search for God that the spirit seeks. Death frees us from such restrictions and opens new life for us. Some people speak of death as a moment when we make our final 'yes' to the Lord and accept him by an ultimate choice. But speculations shall go on and men shall seek answers to the question of the death of the body. For us, Sister Death is a reality of life. It finishes our pilgrimage on earth and brings us to the reality of community life with the Trinity. The mind of man cannot even imagine the wonders in store for us at that moment. Living or dying, we are the Father's in all things.

You are not in the dark, Brothers, that the day should catch you off guard like a thief. No, all of you are children of light and of the day. We belong neither to darkness nor to night; therefore let us not be asleep like the rest, but awake and sober! Sleepers sleep by night and drunkards drink by night. We who live by day must be alert, putting on faith and love as a breastplate and the hope of salvation as a helmet. God has not destined us for wrath but for acquiring salvation through our Lord Jesus Christ. He died for us, that all of us, whether awake or asleep, together might live with him. Therefore, comfort and upbuild one another, as indeed you are doing.

1 Thessalonians 5: 4 - 11

How wise is the man who is always ready, standing prepared for the day of the Lord. How helpful is Sister Death who reminds us of the importance of life.

ACTION

Following the Franciscan way of life requires that we identify with the poor, with the 'little ones' in our world. Most especially shall we be concerned with those poor overlooked by others. The poor of the statistics, who lack the money and power to achieve success. The unemployed who subsist on unemployment insurance or welfare checks. The children who never see green grass and live in a world of fear and insecurity. The over 6 million people whose lives are controlled by alcohol and other millions controlled by drugs of various sorts. The American Indian who has little say even on his own Reservation. The people who are oppressed because business is more concerned with profits than with people. The list is endless. But hidden beneath all the statistics and reports are people who are suffering.

A Franciscan ought to know and try to understand the

bigger picture about poverty and need. But the spirit of Francis always comes back to the person who is hurting or in need. We get to know the Juans and Joses, the Chief Running Clouds and Roosevelt Browns, the Lolitas and Sallys and all the nameless people who need someone to be for them. We walk with them; we experience their hurt and pain; we are one with them in loneliness. We listen to the Peters and Marys who are in emotional turmoil. We listen to the agonies of unwed, pregnant girls who are so afraid of what is happening to them. We reach out to the neighbor who hates anyone who is different. We do much of this on a person-to-person basis so that each man might know he is loved. This does not eliminate the possibility of organizing in order to help. But our own inner attitude is always directed to a very personal concern and awareness.

Moreover, we will work to moving beyond the 'now' problem and try to search out the causes of the problems of poverty or hunger or neglect. We do this because it is important for the individual person to find and deal with the causes of his need. We will clothe and comfort and feed and listen, but we will also strive to eliminate the causes of injustice and oppression. This is the harder task. Immediate needs are easier to meet than to tackle the bigger issues. There is a more immediate response and a feeling of success when someone gives a delighted "thank you" for a jacket or food basket. In some ways these things can be self-seeking instead of being truly points of Christian love. As Franciscans we are called to do both things—to deal with the immediate need, whatever it may be, but also to try to deal with the causes of that need so that we might change things. If we were alone in our efforts, we might simply give up. If our fraternity life is what it ought to be, we shall not be alone. We may not always see the end of our efforts, but we cannot refrain from trying. We shall try to bring our faith, our hope, our joy and our love to the needs of people. Perhaps a Spanish proverb sums up our aims in this regard:

If you give a man a fish, you feed him for today.
If you teach him how to fish, he need never go hungry
again.

Every fraternity is a combination of people. People who
have the know-how in doing things, who can organize and be
active in the work with the problems of people; those who
share in the work load in accomplishing all of this; those who
besiege the Lord for the help we need to be his instruments
and not forget Him. There are dreamers with their vision;
doers with the work of their hands; pray-ers who keep us in
touch with the Lord. When a Franciscan fraternity works
together, each member doing what he can, then our action
will make sense. When each member appreciates and shares
that appreciation with the others, then we will also be
a community aware of itself and its strength. Francis never
intended that we should hide, ostrich-like, from the problems
of people. It is the world of our Father and his people are
involved. We must be responsive or lose some of the fullness
of our calling.

In all the talk about 'love' in today's world, we might
get the false impression that it is something we just fall into.
But the love we speak of does not really look for success in
our work, even while we work hard to achieve it. The love
we speak of does not shy away from risks in helping others,
for we certainly do not always have answers. The love we
speak of shall be aware that we may be hurt and have to
suffer if we are going to care about people, but we cannot
stop trying for that reason. Our love will ultimately demand
everything of us and that is what we seek, so that it is no
longer I who lives, but Christ lives in me.

With the growth of love there comes a development in
creative spontaneity. In St Francis it was immense,
secure, powerful, enveloping, attractive and ever-vic-
torious. Anchored on the solid rock of true love, on

the immense expanse of love, he feared nothing in this world. "Perfect love casts out all fear." He never feared his instinctive spontaneity, for love always kept it in bounds; he never feared norms or laws, because love always turned them into freedom for him. Thus, the Little Poor Man was able to be faithful to duty and to law without becoming a slave to them. He could be spontaneous without being victim to arbitrariness or anarchy, without falling into mediocrity or superficiality.

How far we pilgrims still have to trudge before reaching that level of love which thus brings back paradise! But let us convince ourselves, and right here and now, that this is really the spirituality of St Francis, that this is the road which leads to intense life with God, in universal love and in making the horizontal and vertical converge.

. . . Because he had reached such heights of love and of the attitudes that love breeds, Francis could resolve the tensions between person and group, between the individual and society, between pre-established norms and formulas and spontaneity. For this reason Francis enjoyed such security while moving in the midst of enormous crisis in the Church of his time. This is why he could always be peaceful, tactful, meek, courteous with his own and with high dignitaries, with the harsh attitudes of the world, with society; all the time drawing men and institutions into renewed life with God. This is why he could be a Catholic without infuriating those who were not. This is why he could hold dialogue with the Sultan of Egypt.

Our life with God, Koser O.F.M., 87 - 88

The love that moves us must be a gentle love that is firm

and solidly based on faith in Jesus. Our love will express itself in the manner the gospel demands. Our calling to follow Francis means that we shall be revolutionaries, ready and eager for change, but not rebels who would discard any good thing that stands in the way of self-seeking. We are called to treasure the heritage of our past, our personal past, our Franciscan past and the past of the people of God. But we are also awake and sensitive to the good things that the present offers, ready to embrace the things that will move us to greater love and/or understanding of Jesus and his gospel. We can understand the position of someone who may disagree with us, without losing our own convictions or sense of direction. We can be sharp and perceptive in pinpointing the sores in society without becoming the enemy of society. Above all, we can get down to the essentials without becoming embroiled in controversies about non-essentials. We shall walk through this world like the peace of God and not as a wrathful people. We will be troubled by injustice and oppression, but we will avoid becoming a new kind of oppressor by our actions or attitudes. Our model for reaching out to people shall reflect our imitation of the Father in the Parable of the prodigal son, always waiting to forgive and embrace. Others may exceed us in organization; others may surpass us in the press coverage they receive for works accomplished; others may be wiser in the way they react to needs. But no one should ever surpass Franciscans in the gentle compassion and acceptance that we give to one another. No one should ever feel unwanted after he has been in touch with us. Like Francis, we shall try to give dignity to every person; acceptance to the outcast; love to the unlovable—so that this may be a moment of their own desire to be all they can be.

There will always be a struggle in the 'how-to-do-it' of action for Jesus. We must face primary responsibilities and recognize them as apostolic actions. Marriage, priesthood, religious life, single life in the world, studies, work—all of

these are already areas of service to God's people. We are
committed to loving wife and husband, brother and sister,
neighbor and fellow worker just as fully as we reach out in
love to the person with some special need outside of this
group. There will be a tension trying to decide. But such a
tension shall bring us to prayer and to Jesus for help. Sometimes our most important action, at a given moment, is to
that child of ours who needs us rather than to a committee
that requires time and service of us. We must be sensitive to
all of this so that our action is not an escape from our
response-ability to those close to us. We must do the one
without neglecting the other. Above all, what we have to
offer others as Christians must never be simply our own
human love. It must be the love of Christ channeling through
us to touch others. That requires prayerfulness of us. It
requires taking time for the Lord, lest we be empty vessels
sounding our mournful cry in the wilderness of a life empty
of faith in Jesus.

THE HOLY SPIRIT

In another time the Holy Spirit was known as the 'forgotten God.' Today he is not only remembered, he is
welcomed into our lives and seen to be the 'breath' that
keeps us Christians alive. Both Christ and St Paul (in his
epistles) were liberal in their words about the Holy Spirit.
Our own 're-discovery' is simply an awakening on our part
and not a lack of teaching on the part of Jesus or his
followers.

Jesus, on the night before his death on the Cross, spoke
about the Spirit to his apostles.

> This much I have told you while I was still
> with you. The Paraclete, the Holy Spirit whom
> the Father will send in my name, will instruct
> you in everything, and remind you of all that

I told you.

John 14: 25 - 26

When the Paraclete comes, the Spirit of truth who comes from the Father—and whom I myself will send from the Father—he will bear witness on my behalf. You must bear witness as well for you have been with me from the beginning.

John 15: 26 - 27

I have much more to tell you, but you cannot bear it now. When he comes, however, being the Spirit of truth, he will guide you to all truth. He will not speak on his own, but will speak only what he hears, and will announce to you the things to come. In doing this he will give glory to me, because he will have received from me what he will announce to you.

John 16: 12 - 14

Jesus makes it plain that one thing the Spirit shall do is to help us know the truth. The Spirit's coming will assist us in understanding the truth that Jesus wants us to know. His coming will reveal things about Jesus when we are ready to receive them. The strengthening of faith is in the hands of the Spirit. Moreover, we are expected to bear witness to this truth. The Spirit shall strengthen us to bear witness to Jesus. We shall not be alone in trying to give witness. The Spirit shall be with us so that we can give viable witness to the truth. Jesus is clear about this as he speaks to his apostles about their mission and how the power for mission will come from the Spirit:

You will receive power when the Holy Spirit comes down on you; then you are to be my witnesses in Jerusalem, throughout Judea and Samaria, yes, even to the ends of the earth.

Acts of the Apostles, 1:8

The truth of this promise is made clear in the description of the first Pentecost.

> When the day of Pentecost came it found them gathered in one place. Suddenly from up in the sky there came a noise like a strong, driving wind which was heard all through the house where they were seated. Tongues as of fire appeared, which parted and came to rest on each of them. All were filled with the Holy Spirit. They began to express themselves in foreign tongues and make bold proclamations as the Spirit prompted them.

> . . . Peter stood up and addressed them: ". . . it is what Joel the prophet spoke of:

> 'It shall come to pass in the last days, says God, that I will pour out a portion of my spirit on all mankind; Your sons and daughters shall prophesy, your young men shall see visions and your old men shall dream dreams. Yes, even on my servants and handmaids I will pour out a portion of my spirit in those days, and they shall prophesy. I will work wonders in the heavens above and signs on the earth below;' "

> Acts 2: 1 - 4; 14 - 19

This task of proclamation joined to the expression of the power of the Spirit still belongs to the people of God. We have the same Spirit teaching and strengthening us. If we are to speak the message clearly and without confusion, we have need of the Spirit so that we might speak and live the truth of the gospel.

> Eye has not seen, ear has not heard, nor has it so much as dawned on man what God has prepared for those who love him. Yet God has revealed this wisdom to us through the Spirit. The Spirit scrutinizes all matters,

even the deep things of God. Who, for example, knows a man's innermost self but the man's own spirit within him? Similarly, no one knows what lies at the depths of God but the Spirit of God. The Spirit we have received is not the world's spirit but God's Spirit, helping us to recognize the gifts he has given us.

1 Corinthians 2: 9 - 13

Clearly the Spirit is present in us to teach us the truth and to strengthen us for witness. In the pursuit of these two aims, the Spirit can operate well only if we are receptive to his inspirations. Once again we need to review our lives to see how receptive we are. If, for example, there is a barrier of resentment, refusal to forgive hurts or jealousies in our inner heart, the Spirit will be hindered in his working in our lives. For us to expect the peace of the Lord or his healing reconciliation to take place when our hearts are at war with another is to fool ourselves. The barrier of animosity goes counter to the Spirit of Love. If we are lazy, smug, absolutely self-centered and complacent, the Spirit will find us unaware of the demands of his inspiration. We won't even be 'awake' to hear him since we are only awake to ourselves. Such a lack of openness to the Spirit keeps us from real joy and peace as we bask in some artificial 'peace' of our own making.

The gifts of the Holy Spirit are ours to use. The Spirit has been given. But our realization and acceptance of that fact is not always present in us. Again, the special sense of the beatitude, of being an "anawim," a poor one, is vitally important. When he speaks about these gifts of the Spirit, Paul also makes clear that they are meant for building up the community. Whether it is the gift of teaching or prophesying; speaking in tongues or serving, the gifts are to build up and unify the community of believers.

Since you have set your hearts on spiritual gifts, try to

be rich in those that build up the church. This means that the man who speaks in a tongue should pray for the gift of interpretation. If I pray in a tongue my spirit is at prayer but my mind contributes nothing. What is my point here? I want to pray with my spirit, and also to pray with my mind as well. If your praise of God is solely with the spirit, how will the one who does not comprehend be able to say "Amen" to your thanksgiving? He will not know what you are saying. You will be uttering praise very well indeed, but the other man will not be helped. Thank God, I speak in tongues more than any of you, but in the Church I would rather say five intelligible words to instruct others than ten thousand words in a tongue.

. . . What do we propose, Brothers? When you assemble one has a psalm, another some instruction to give, still another a revelation to share; one speaks in a tongue, another interprets. All well and good so long as everything is done with a constructive purpose.

1 Corinthians 14: 12 - 19; 26

The gifts of the Spirit are meant to build up the community of believers. In a sense, they are not our own to hoard or hide. They are meant to be used for the sake of the church. Whenever the gifts of the Spirit lead to exclusivism or even worse, deliberate exclusion of people, then something is wrong. The Spirit always wishes to unite and draw together those who believe. As splendid as the variety of gifts is, each is meant to build up the unity-in-diversity of the Body of Christ. As Paul speaks of it, he compares it to the many parts of the body, all different, yet each contributing to the health of the one body. The same Spirit works in each of us but the gifts may be different.

There are different gifts but the same Spirit; there are

different ministries but the same Lord; there are different works but the same God who accomplishes all of them in everyone. To each person the manifestation of the Spirit is given for the common good. To one the spirit gives wisdom in discourse, to another the power to express knowledge. Through the Spirit one receives faith; by the same Spirit another is given the gift of healing, and still another miraculous powers. Prophecy is given to one; to another power to distinguish one spirit from another. One receives the gift of tongues, another that of interpreting the tongues. But it is one and the same Spirit who produces all these gifts distributing them to each as he wills.

1 Corinthians 12: 4 - 11

One important criteria for discerning the Spirit in a man is to see if the gifts are used for personal glory or for building up the community. Look to the freedom that is present, for the Spirit always respects the individual. Where the Spirit of the Lord is, there is freedom. (2 Corinthians 3:17)

The Spirit shall also draw us to a deeper intimacy with the Trinity. Scripture speaks especially of being 'bonded' to the Father. It is the Spirit that makes us able to cry out to God and call him "Father."

All who are led by the Spirit of God are sons of God. You did not receive a spirit of slavery leading you back into fear, but a spirit of adoption through which we cry out "Abba" (i.e. "Father") The Spirit himself gives witness with our spirit that we are children of God. But if we are children, we are heirs as well; heirs of God, heirs with Christ, if only we suffer with him so as to be glorified with him.

Romans 8: 14 - 17

Our Lord taught us to pray by teaching us about our

Father and telling us to call him "Father." As members of the family of God, we are to resemble the complete dedication and love for each other that Father, Son and Spirit have in the life of the Trinity. None of us are so naive in our faith as to expect to be able to do this alone. Jesus sent his Spirit to enable us to live this way. Without the Spirit we shall do nothing. With the Spirit, all things are possible for us.

Paul himself gives us some points of direction in helping us recognize the presence of the Spirit. He contrasts the results between absence and presence of the Spirit in the life of the Christian.

My Brothers, remember that you have been called to live in freedom—but not a freedom that gives free reign to the flesh. Out of love, place yourselves at one another's service. The whole law has found its fulfillment in this one saying: "You shall love your neighbor as yourself." If you go on biting and tearing one another to pieces, take care! You will end up in mutual destruction!

My point is that you should live in accord with the spirit and you will not yield to the cravings of the flesh. The flesh lusts against the spirit and the spirit against the flesh; the two are directly opposed. This is why you do not do what your will intends. If you are guided by the spirit, you are not under the law. It is obvious what proceeds from the flesh; lewd conduct, impurity, licentiousness, idolatry, sorcery, hostilities, bickering, jealousy, outbursts of rage, selfish rivalries, dissensions, factions, envy, drunkenness, orgies, and the like. I warn you, as I have warned you before; those who do such things will not inherit the kingdom of God!

In contrast, the fruit of the spirit is love, joy, peace, patient endurance, kindness, generosity, faith, mildness, and chastity. Against such there is no law! Those who belong to Christ Jesus have crucified their flesh with its passions and desires. Since we live by the spirit, let us follow the spirit's lead. Let us never be boastful or challenging or jealous toward one another.

. . . May I never boast of anything but the cross of our Lord Jesus Christ! Through it, the world has been crucified to me and I to the world. It means nothing whether one is circumcised or not. All that matters is that one is created anew. Peace and mercy on all who follow this rule of life . . .

Galatians 5: 13 - 26; 6: 14 - 16

Among the followers of Francis, the fruits of the Holy Spirit must be clearly seen. Of special importance, it seems to me, are two of those fruits, namely, patient endurance and generosity. Both of these require a great deal of faith. To each must be added an abundant quantity of mildness (gentleness). There are so many times that fraternity life can become frustrating. People do not always respond to well-intentioned ideas. Not everyone agrees with projects that are planned. Sometimes we sense a resistance in Franciscans to letting loose of pet ideas for the sake of the Lord. Often we seek our own personal success rather than the will of the Father. It seems to me that a Franciscan who is really moved by the Spirit, shall approach all such problems with a patient gentleness. No lambasting of people, but a gentle and firm urging. No condemnation of another's action (no matter how wrong) but a gentle acceptance a la the Father of the prodigal son. A gentle willingness to suffer for beliefs when there is misunderstanding or misinterpretation of motives. A patient willingness not to force one's ideas on another who walks in a different place than our own. Generosity in forgiving personal hurts caused by a friend. Generosity and patience in not being able to solve problems, especially for those who are close to us—but ready and present to walk in their pain and share their burden. Gentleness will require a firm rejection of things that would destroy the community without destroying the person who acts this way. The delicate and absolutely total demands of the Spirit will never be fulfilled without the Spirit. As we grow more open to this Spirit and less concerned about ourselves, the Spirit will lead us to places and people and situations that we had never dreamed about. There we shall share the riches of the Spirit in gentle, generous, patient and joy-full readiness to be all we can in that situation.

Francis of Assisi responded in this manner to the Spirit. He listened to the Spirit and chose the whole gospel as his way of life. Never did he seek to water it down, yet he had a gentle understanding of those who found it difficult. The Spirit gave Francis a special awareness of the love of the Father and led him to a life of hope and faith and love. The same Spirit calls us to that same commitment using His gifts in our lives. He will teach us what we need to know and he will strengthen us to follow the gospel of Jesus. The impossible dream of Francis and Christ is no longer out of reach for us, for the Spirit will help us. The need of today's world for this kind of commitment and this kind of faith is clear. We need people of vision who believe that the Spirit is at work among us. We need people with the seed of hope because they recognize the power of the Spirit at work. We need a people in love with God and man because they recognize the power of the Spirit at work within us. This realization of God's abundant love, lavished in Christ and powered by the Spirit leads us to pray:

May the God of our Lord Jesus Christ, the Father of glory, grant you a spirit of wisdom and insight to know him clearly. May he enlighten your innermost vision that you may know the great hope to which he has called you, the wealth of his glorious heritage to be distributed among the members of the church, and the immeasurable scope of his power in us who believe. It is like the strength he showed in raising Christ from the dead and seating him at his right hand in heaven, high above every principality, power, virtue and domination, and every name that can be given in this age or in the age to come.

Ephesians 1: 17 - 21

. . . and I pray that he will bestow on you gifts in keeping with the riches of his glory. May he strengthen you inwardly through the working of his Spirit. May Christ dwell in your hearts through faith, and may charity be the root and foundation of your life. Thus you will be able to grasp fully, with all the holy ones, the breadth and length and height and depth of Christ's love, and experience this love which surpasses all knowledge, so that you may attain to the fullness of God himself.

To him whose power now at work in us can do immeasurably more than we ask or imagine—to him be glory in the Church and in Christ Jesus through all generations, world without end, Amen.

Ephesians 3: 16 - 21

18. Forever and Today

No ONE CAN REASONABLY HOPE to be able to touch on every point of the spiritual life in a single book. The only book that does that is the Bible. Perhaps that is why Francis was practical enough to take it as his rule of life. Our exploration into this Franciscan way of life has simply been a short journey through some of the important elements in following Francis. We know of the Father's call. We know of our deep need for faith in this Father. We know that Jesus is the way to the Father, the one who shall teach us about the Father. We know that the Spirit sent by Jesus shall teach us what we need to know and move us to act as Christians. Men and women who wish to follow the Franciscan way of life come to a point where they must make this decision for themselves. Instruction, formation, prayer and action ought to help in making this decision. But it is still a deeply personal decision and an important one, for it will affect the whole of life. Profession of the Franciscan way of life means that you deliberately, freely and publicly commit yourself to follow the gospel in the spirit of St Francis. It is one way of deepening and/or renewing the promises you made to Jesus at baptism. The Franciscan way of life provides the help of a special community joined together to give life and breathe to the gospel. It is not magic nor is it always simple and easy. But it joins together people intent and concerned about being a gospel people. As a member of our Franciscan community you are no longer alone in this search. You are joined with men and women, young and old throughout the world who share your search. We walk together through a some-times antagonistic world; but there is strength and support in our unity.

St Francis does not add new reasons for sinning. Profession in the Third Order of St Francis does not bind under pain of sin. It is much more a call to generosity than any kind of imposition of legalisms. If we fail to keep the commitment of our profession we will not achieve the goal that is promised to us, the perfection to which the Father calls us. But this failure is more a personal loss than a matter of sin, unless our failures also violate some requirement of God's law or laws of the Church. Obviously, the person who would make this profession and then ignore the responsibilities while seeking all the privileges would be foolish indeed. He would show an ignorance of the Franciscan way of life. To continue under such circumstances would be to live a lie. We have a serious responsibility to one another to avoid any such thing in our fraternity life.

Profession of the Franciscan way of life requires a total commitment to the gospel. Ordinarily this is done within the framework of fraternity life. The very real needs of a gospel people must be met. Coming together often to share ex-periences in living the gospel; to share reflection on the Scriptures; to pray with and for one another—these are essentials to full Franciscan living. In particular cases it may be possible to allow some leeway in this regard, but it is always an exception and never the rule. We need one another both for support and for practical criticism on the road to change. Perhaps we might look at some of the things that are essential in our Franciscan way of life.

Our living of the gospel life is patterned on the spirit in which St Francis followed the gospel. Francis accepted the gospel just as it is. He made no attempt to change it to fit his convenience nor to deny the possibility of its demands. He simply and plainly took it as it is and tried to live it. If we would follow Francis we must try to do the same. Our whole life will be spent learning how to do this—but that is precisely why we make a profession of this way of life. To take the whole gospel seriously is what we profess to do. Our personal surrender to the Lord in faith will be a part of our way to the Lord. Our hope that the Spirit will bring us to perfection is also a part of our equipment. The journey of Francis in seeking this perfection shall stimulate us to do likewise. His joy will draw us to greater efforts in our attempts to be a gospel people.

The very nature of human beings is such that there are many barriers that exist within us, keeping us from the goal of union with Jesus. Day after day we are faced with choices and decisions that will reveal the direction our life is taking. We will hopefully go on discovering new ways of seeing things, new attitudes and approaches to situations. The need for constant renewal and change is a part of life for the Franciscan. By our profession we accept the responsibility to keep on changing ourselves so that we are more responsive to the Spirit. There will always be attic corners of our self that we discover we have kept for ourselves. They will have to be handed over to the Lord. Again, we will experience our need for the power of the Spirit as we seek to become an instrument in the hands of the Lord. Conversion is always happening if we are really aware of the Lord. The demand that we be brothers to one another, that we recognize the beauty and wonder of God not only in creation but also in people is not always easy. Not everyone is likeable nor does everyone think we are so likeable. Conversion will require facing the reality of our feelings while groping to bring them in accord with gospel requirements. We can't get lost in the beauty of creation and be blind to the goodness in modern day lepers. We are called to brotherhood and that will require true self-discipline; a capacity for compassion; a desire for reconciliation; and a great dose of generosity. It can be done, and we believe it will be done, because we are called to give such an example of brotherhood through our

Franciscan calling.

At the center of everything; in the middle of our life; at the core of our heart there can be only one foundation stone, the cornerstone of the gospel, Jesus Christ. His is the pattern of life we choose to follow. He is the one who shall make it possible for us to grow in Him. He will lead us both to the revelations of glory on Mt Tabor ("It is good for us to be here!") and to the agonies of Mt Calvary ("My God, why have you forsaken me!"). The circle of life shall embrace both of these, death and resurrection, in an often repeated cycle. In all things, Christ is the head, the source of life. Nothing and no one can replace him in our life. Francis serves as a special messenger, but Francis brings us to Christ in the same way that Mary, the Virgin Mother does. For the followers of Francis, there is a special love for the poor and crucified Christ. Above all we shall witness to the fact that suffering and death are not ends in themselves. They are the way to life. But Jesus followed the way of clinging to the Father's will in every situation, even in death and suffering. We Franciscans find special meaning in that. Christ came to us in littleness and departed from this world empty-handed. He meant to teach us the value of littleness. This mark of Jesus is especially precious to Franciscans and colors our approach to Christ. Some see him as king; others see him as the great teacher; still others see him as the miracle worker. We accept all of these ideas about the Lord too. But first and foremost he is our Brother, poor, little and lover of those who are poor and little. This is the kind of special message we bring to the world. A sort of counter sign to the mad scramble for wealth and profits that distorts the vision of so many people. We are the "little ones," oftentimes poor; almost always out-organized; often making foolish mistakes about worldly things; but always deeply trusting of our Father and secure in the power of the Spirit. We are a people whose loyalty to the Church reflects that of Francis. In his age the Church structure left much to be desired. Yet

Francis remained dedicated to the Church, at one with her; trying to recapture the beauty that lay hidden under crusts of wealth and power and immorality, for she is the Body of Christ. We too shall be loyal today. We shall be loyal when we must work with reluctant pastors or enthusiastic ones; with progressives who shock or conservatives who are holding back; with people who work hard or with those who like the headlines and hate the work. We will be consistently loyal right where we are, persistent in the face of any kind of frustration and failure. Always trying to assist in the work of proclaiming the gospel here and now for the people of our world.

The prayer of St Francis calls for many qualities of love. But a special quality of Franciscans must always be their willingness to work for peace and reconciliation. There are all degrees and levels of this work. But Franciscans, by their very calling, will not simply sit around discussing peace and reconciliation. At most, this is only a beginning point. The gospel does not call simply for discussion, but for action. We must be willing to be personally involved in creating the climate for peace. If we must forgive someone who has destroyed our reputation or only muddied it, then we shall forgive. If the lines of communication are broken in a friendship, we will not rest until we can find some way of opening communication again. If black man and white man and Indian and Spanish-Americans are warring with each other, we will not see reconciliation as hopeless. There too we shall work for peace even though we may never see it arrive in our lifetime. The Franciscan is not committed to success in what he tries to do. He is absolutely committed to try however and to try again and again as people of hope will always do. We shall try a thousand different avenues to peace, but we shall never say it is impossible. We shall stand for life. This too may be a cause for tension and conflict. But we cannot look for an artificial peace that does away with God's gift of life whether through abortion or mercy killing or anything in between. We seek the peace called *shalom* which requires a wholeness in the heart of man. No man at enmity with God or his neighbor can know real shalom. Peace shall be the sign of life among the members of the fraternity and they shall be support and strength in the struggle for peace and reconciliation. Above all else we shall seek that shalom in our own heart, working to be at peace with God and our fellow man and ourselves. Such a demand to be a peacemaker shall bring us to the Lord in serious, constant, communal and liturgical prayer. The God who calls us is also the one who shall transform us by the power of his Spirit. Unless we 'stand still' before God, really give him honest and undivided attention in prayer, we shall be broken bells giving uncertain sounds. We need to pray alone. We need to pray together. We need to pray with the community of believers whenever they gather. And most of all, we need to pray in Eucharist, where the Lord comes in the form of bread, to be our strength. To pray well is to learn how much we need the Lord. To pray well is to learn to understand our neighbor as God does. To pray well is to be always ready to be present to anyone who needs us.

When Francis faced the reality of God and chose to accept the Father totally, it is said that he went singing into the forest. The true follower of Francis and the gospel will be a person of joy. As we grow in the belief that the Father really loves us, knows us individually by name, would do anything to save us even when we stray, who will forgive us no matter what happens, who wants us to have life in abundance—to grow in that belief is to grow in joy. We are someone of worth and dignity, not because we are so great in ourselves, but because God does not love junk. We are certainly worth more than sparrows or birds or flowers. Jesus said that to us. I am embraced by God. What a joy, then, to be a pilgrim in his world, commissioned by the Spirit to share the message of the gospel, called by the Father to intimacy with the Trinity. It's almost unbelievable that I should be so loved.

So I want to be free of things to be able to respond to this love and come to the life and joy of the Lord. A joy that is pressed down and running over. How freeing it is to know that my security lies in someone who will never stop loving me, never cease seeking my good. Possessions become a nuisance if they possess me. So I try to travel light through my Father's world, using the gifts he is sure to give me. How we will love this world of our Father's even while we look forward to the homecoming he has in store for us.

When we walk in the way of self-giving and generosity, our deepest concern will be with those overlooked by others. The people who may often be ungrateful for the help that is given. The people who are easily hidden behind statistics on reports. The people who have no power nor hope of rewarding you. The people whose case seems hopeless. The people who have given up hope. The people who will waste our time. The people who may never change and give us some promise of success. Such as these are our people. We will care about them and respect them so that they may be able to respect themselves. We shall not be saviors to them, standing above them on pious pedestals. We shall be brothers to them, walking where they walk, hand in hand. Here is where we shall experience the pain of the little ones and become little ourselves. Here we will be stripped of pretense and vast projects. Here is the place of simplicity when the only gift we have is the gift of ourself. Like Jesus, we shall plunge into the world of the people around us without clinging to personal dignity. Instead we shall identify with those we serve and become like them in everything but sin, so that we might imitate the Son of God.

The vision of Francis of Assisi is as alive and real and needed in our day as at any time in history. Our need for one another in a community dedicated to the gospel is a crying need of today. Our need for openness to the Spirit is a clear need of today when problems seem insurmountable. Our need to be little brothers to each other is obvious since

being 'big brother' hasn't worked. Our need to center our
lives on our relationship to Christ in faith is clearly needed
in a world of lonely, bored and alienated people. The vision
of Francis cries out to men and women today as never
before. The need for meaning that only the cross can give is
vitally needed in our understanding of love. Wherever we
look we can see how a lonely world is in need of understanding the incarnation of Jesus. We need to be witnesses to
the good news that God is alive! That God loves every single
one of us! That Jesus is alive and lives in us! That God is our
Father! That the little ones shall have the gospel preached to
them and the blind will see and the lame walk and men will
change and turn to God! We are meant to be witnesses to
hope, for Jesus is true to his word. We are meant to console
the suffering and bear the burdens of those whose yoke is
heavy. We are meant to forgive one another whatever needs
forgiveness so that we might be forgiven by the Father. We
are meant to praise the Lord constantly but especially at the
Eucharist. In all that we are and in all that we become, we
are meant to show the world that the gospel is not just good
reading, but is *thee* way of life.

Franciscans, like all good Christians, must always celebrate
life and love. Somewhere, in the deepest recesses of our
heart, there is a longing to be possessed by the Lord. We
desire to be so taken hold of that there would be no release.
So loved that love would never cease. So full of joy that no
sadness could ever destroy it. So convinced of the truth that
no lies could ever turn us away from Him who is the truth.
So intimate with Life that we would be one with Him. So
free in all of this because the great Lover would lead us to be
ourselves like no one else could ever do. For this, then, let
us pray:

> As the mountain stream is fed by melting snows
> it grows and deepens. As the warm sun melts the
> snow and feeds the stream, it becomes a thundering

river, galloping down the mountain side in a flash of
white, running water.

Melt my hardness, Lord,
and the coldness of my love.
Let me be a roaring stream, fed and nourished
by the melting snows of pride and selfishness,
to become a galloping stream
of dedication and compassion,
of love and sharing,
running to the sea
that is living water —
running to you, O Lord.

Amen.